Silence

Silence

The Currency of Power

Edited by

Maria-Luisa Achino-Loeb

Berghahn Books
New York • Oxford

First published in 2006 by

Berghahn Books
www.berghahnbooks.com

Library of Congress Cataloging-in-Publication Data

Silence : the currency of power / edited by Maria-Luisa Achino-Loeb.
p. cm.
Includes bibliographical references and index.
ISBN 1-84545-130-9 -- ISBN 1-84545-131-7 (pbk.)
1. Silence. 2. Power (Social sciences) I. Achino-Loeb, Maria Luisa.

BJ1499.S5S55 2005
302.2--dc22 2005047342

British Library Cataloguing in Publication Data

A catalogue record for this book is available from the British Library
Printed in the United States on acid-free paper

Contents

List of Figures and Tables

Acknowledgements

This approach to silence has been in gestation for quite some time and has benefited from the input of many people. Primary among them are the students of N.Y.U. / Gallatin; students whose unabashed skepticism kept silence grounded; students whose taste for the esoteric allowed silence to soar. I also wish to recognize the many colleagues and friends who have read it in its various incarnations, in particular, Laurie Schneider Adams, Patricia Antoniello, Gloria Levitas, Setha Low, Frances Rothstein, Nina Glick Schiller, Gerald Sider and Alisse Waterston: their critique and support have strengthened my resolve. Finally, a special recognition goes to Larry M. Loeb whose generous and solicitous assistance has helped smooth many of the kinks of this project.

The book began to take its present shape at the 2000 AAA meetings in San Francisco, when a session by the same title received a very warm reception, indeed. I am grateful to Pauline Gardiner Barber, William O. Beeman, James W. Fernandez, and Ann E. Kingsolver, all original participants in that session, for agreeing to embark on the long and only partially charted waters of the edited-volume journey and to Susan E. Cook, Robin E. Sheriff, and Gerald Sider for agreeing to join this journey on silence.

The rich ethnographic material and considerable insights brought on board by each of these contributors have made it possible for our volume to tackle critical theoretical ground: in brief, by poking holes in some long cherished controversies that keep resurfacing in our discipline under different labels, but that involve divergent takes on the source of reliability of knowledge and on the role of the observer in dealing with it. What is interesting about our volume is that it gathers the work of anthropologists who have stood on opposite sides of some of these controversies. And what we are saying is that it's no good trying to pretend that we can arrive at a foolproof place of authenticity: all observation is indeed slanted or, minimally, partial—as is all experience, for that matter. But that does not mean that it is not usable as source of knowledge. What we *can* do as anthropologists, with our perhaps simple-minded trust in observation, is document the behaviors that actively suppress aspects of reality in favor of others. The study of silence, we claim, takes us there. It helps us trace the unobtrusive development of ideologies and, conversely, it helps us voice the ideological foundation of meaning: a good start for the analysis of power.

Thank you, to one and all and to the memory of Eric R. Wolf, who first started me on this journey. It's been a trip!

Introduction

Silence as the Currency of Power

Maria-Luisa Achino-Loeb

This book is intended as an exploration of silence as analytic domain and as window on the elusive and overt roots of power.

Silence is wide. It lures our anthropological imagination beyond imputed origins of speech to a whooshing, plopping, slithering universe devoid of exegetical consciousness. Lacking interpreters, experience cannot be parsed into selective absences, rather it collapses into absolute simultaneity; presence and absence become one. Only when *ouch* became phonemic could it have pierced the silence, morphing a sonorous universe into discrete items of significance.

Beyond human communication, then, silence is meaningless as a discrete concept, separate from life or from existence, but not meaningless as a metaphor of power, for it serves as avenue for giving voice to unencumbered experience. Perhaps that is why poets and visionaries have dipped their visions of human creativity in one or another dimension of silence; as Luis Borges does with his Dantesque fantasy of descent into the secret space of *The Aleph*, where human existence can be experienced as coterminous with all other existence (Cardinal 2000); or as Beckett (1954) does with his play on speechlessness, where the audience is drawn into constructing meaning for characters endlessly waiting for meaningful completion in a putative Godot. Perhaps that is why some aspects of silence have been used for practices whose goal is to reach beyond the human condition (Rinpoche 1993).

Confusion—purposeful or otherwise—among the referential domains of silence is a direct result of its connection to power as currency for its exercise. The object of this book is to verbalize the incremental and inevitable grounds of such connection, and hence to argue that the study of silence is central to understanding the more elusive aspects of power. Its guiding premise is that silence, while universal in its form as perceived absence, is indicative of repressed, unobtrusive presence and functionally tied to the context.

In anthropology we have tackled periodically the topic of silence and its contingent meaning. Since the 1960's, research on Apache speech patterns has focused on the situational, strategic, dimensions of silence (Basso 1970). All along there have been attempts to demonstrate how silence can be analyzed as an integral part of speech, with several tries at devising an ethnography of silence (Tannen and Saville-Troike, eds. 1985). One theme, tying these approaches, is that the power of silence resides in its inherent ambiguity. And its ambiguity stems from the universal acceptance of silence as a form of withholding, hence as a kind of absence and, simultaneously, the understanding that such withholding or absence exists only in the ear of the listeners—to paraphrase a common adage—who willingly or willfully ignore or veil the pregnant presence encompassed by each instance of silence. Perhaps that is why silence is so slippery as a concept; why it is so hard to find a good "fit" between the experience of silence and the theories we develop for its analysis (Sheriff 2000).

That the semantic space of silence is marked by the experience of presence disguised as absence has serious consequences for the interjection of self-interest in the perception and communication of meaning: a first step in the realization of power. And *self-interest* in these pages is used as an inclusive term to cover practices supporting the perceived needs of any identified self, in any domain, and from any perspective—the closest analogous application would be the deliberate/conscious and the structural/unconscious attributes that have been attached to class analysis (Lucacs 1968).

Writing on the complexity of the power concept, whose usefulness he sees stalled in various definitional entanglements with the concepts of culture and of ideology, Eric Wolf (1999) elaborates four different modalities of power that run from the potency of the individual, to the manipulation of others directly or contextually, to the very structuring of contexts. Power, it seems, is a particularly slippery concept, available more as metaphor in the aftermath of analyses than as object of the analytic process; leading Foucault, for one, to quip that power does not exist, though his work is all about power (Gordon 1972: 198). Unawed by paradoxes, Wolf plods instead through the verbalization of a complex model for its analysis. While Wolf is mostly concerned with structural power, his multimodal premise is open to constructionist approaches that focus on the constitution of identity, such as Michel Foucault's approach to subjectivity (Hoy 1986). In either case, the crux of the analysis is that power is not an objectifiable entity, rather the result of relational processes.

Resting on Wolf's multimodal approach, this book will argue that silence is a vehicle for the exercise of power in all its modalities. The underlying argument is that silence is implicated in power both in the first instance of experience as a by-product of identity and its selectivity; and as part and parcel of the veiling process that accompanies the wielding of power.

We develop such an argument in two major directions. First we will demonstrate how practices of silence are at the heart of the very experience of any identity as a discrete entity. This will be argued most overtly in the first part of the book where we will both deconstruct the essentializing activity involved in the forging of identity and show its inevitability in the perception of meaning as instances of identity, and where we will also begin to trace some of the consequences of such activity; principal among them, the naturalizing of identity.

Secondly, we will illustrate the many ways in which such unobtrusively naturalized identity is implicated in the attainment of self-interest through the selective suppression of experience involved in power manipulations, whether for purposes of domination or of resistance, as well as it is inherent to the construction of an anthropological reality. Therefore, issues of agency in the construction of subjectivity and difference, the incidence of false consciousness and mystification, as well as the role of the observer in the creation of both will be central to the analysis.

Focusing on silence we straddle the divide between modernist or structuralist and postmodernist or poststructuralist approaches to identity and power, which divide can be seen as unproductive or even gratuitous. In her illuminating critique of the binary opposition between essentialist and constructionist approaches to the analysis of difference and of subjectivity, Diana Fuss (1989) argues that the problem is not the identification of essence, often ascribed critically to modernist notions of subjectivity, but rather why such essence is identified. Critics of essentialism, too, delve in essence every time they identify a unified subject—in her example, women are no less essentialized a category of identity when gender is viewed as constituted after birth than when it is deemed innate.

Just as Fuss, from a poststructuralist perspective, has critiqued the too easy rejection of essence in the search for a deconstructed subjectivity, so Eric Wolf, from a Marxian perspective, has critiqued the unproblematic acceptance of identity, too readily "naturalized" in materialist approaches (2001: 375). We agree with Fuss's position of the ubiquity of essence and with Wolf's urging to problematize identity and argue that it is the process of identity formation itself—with its essentializing activities—that gives us a clue to the elusive sources of power; how power in all its modalities works. And it does so by pointing to the suppression of experience that inheres all perception of salience and to the agency involved in such suppression.

Agency is central, we will argue, because discreteness in identity is achieved through a sleight of hand where actual perceptions are denied in order to underline the perceptions required by the context. It follows that identity cannot be seen as a condition; rather it is an activity that ultimately depends on shades of silence for its successful realization. As such, it is ripe for manipulations at the service of self-interest; where issues of mystification and true versus false consciousness loom large. Hence both a deconstructionist push and a Marxian analytic perspective will underlie facets of our analyses.

The book is divided into three parts.

I A first part, in which the nature of silence as the contrastive substratum of identity with its inherent categorical imperative is presented.
II A second part in which the consequences of this are examined in rich ethnographic detail.
III A third part where the emic and etic dimensions of the process are examined with a focus on the plight of the observer.

However glossed, *silence* is used by contributors to this volume to analyze the wherewithal of power manipulations as they run through verbalizations of self-interest variously marked. Thus we encounter the *silence habitus* shadowing all perception of meaning in terms of identity, but uniquely useful in the construction of essentialized identitites, such as that of race (Achino-Loeb). We have the *linguistic erasures* that accompany the standardization of some speech varieties buttressing the preferred groups in some projects of social domination in postcolonial South Africa (Cook), and its converse, the appeal to free speech, in other projects of social domination in the U.S. context, where the silence-laden language of victimization can help turn neighbors into strangers through selective and *strategic alterity* (Kingsolver). We read about the *cultural censorship* that permits racism to function openly, yet be as openly denied in Brazilian society and by its observers; and, contemporarily, how the silence of the oppressed can take shape and become a source of resistance to disinformation, precisely through reliance on symbolic expressions which work below the radar of public recognition, and go unheeded (Sheriff). We read of the selective *elision* of Philippine women's experience in the anthropological analyses that forge them as victims or heroines, produced by uncritical reliance on theoretical paradigms (Barber). And of the *ruptures* in the social fabric of Newfoundlanders and North Carolinians caught up in the vortex of globalized capital; ruptures only bridgeable by observers willing to act on their knowledge (Sider).

While silence is the necessary condition for the perception of contrast in sound and in meaning—for the privileging of salience and the identification of relevance in potential significance embedding all of us as perceivers/observers (Beeman, Achino-Loeb, Fernandez), it is not a restful condition. The *head notes* of abandoned recollections catch us between the ethnographic imperative of assigning salience and our own sense of alternative, potential relevance (Fernandez).

Silence, the Imperatives of Identity, and the Naturalizing of Power

In the first part of the book the focus is on defining the nature of silence as the substratum of identity. Here the connection among silence, significance, and agency is developed through an analysis of the role of the listener—either audience to a music performance or partner in a dialogic encounter—in fixing the meaning of sound or of speech by means of suppression of variation and foregrounding of the privileged experience. It is because sound must exist in a contrastive fashion in order to be identified and committed to memory that perception is streamlined and channeled by means of suppression of variation.

Silence is the necessary ingredient for our experience of music because it marks the boundaries of what we consider music, for musical sound is such only when framed by rests and pauses. However, rests and pauses do not involve absence of sound, rather they are a withholding of those packets of sound the audience has come to recognize as significant for an experience of music—as the work of John Cage has made clear. Conversely, these same withholdings become carriers of musical meaning when foregrounded in a piece (Beeman). Beeman uses the notions of "ground" and "figure" to trace the waxing and waning of semantic import attached to ambient or intended sound. The import of this is to throw light on the intentionality, hence on the agency involved in the production and reception of sound as music. Or, to put it differently, only those sounds which are privileged as significant are experienced as integral to music. So the identity of musical sound is both marked by silence *and* highly contingent.

In speech this occurs with the perception of phonemic discreteness and with the semantic exchange taking place in speech acts (Achino-Loeb).

In her comprehensive discussion of *language ideology*, Kathryn Woolard (1998) sees it operative, (a) in the connection or the disconnection between language use and ideas about language, (b) in the context specific speech described by ethnographers of speaking, and (c) in the evaluative approaches stemming from standardization processes or from various linguistic conflicts that signal supralinguistic power plays. The theoretical approach to silence developed in this volume embraces the above characterizations, while pushing language ideology one step back from the consideration of speech acts to cover sound and its perception.

According to our analysis, even primal aspects of experience, as is the perception of sound, are products of inadvertent agency, hence open to the whim of the context. For our ability to identify the significance of any one sound depends on our capacity to suppress a host of other sounds which are heard, but remain unremarked as carriers of significance, given the bounds of our linguistic context. To the extent that the perception of phonemic discreteness is the first instance in the potential creation of meaningful utterances, any recognition of meaning in speech is embedded in and depends on a silencing activity. Hence language ideology begins at the level of sound where the perception of significance rests on the ability to suppress a wide range of acoustic cues in favor of those permitted by our linguistic context. Further, this muting capacity is swiftly harnessed in the transferal of meaning, where the intentions of the speakers are central—as Austin (1962) has shown in the case of lies.

Hence meaning is inherently tied to the agency of both speakers and hearers whose intentions and perceptions are key to the communicative capacity of speech.

Phonemes turn out to be a useful anthropological tool for tracing the inherent constructedness of identity and the practices of silence in which it is steeped. For in any identity —as I will argue in Chapter 2— the need for consistency and salience requires isolating contrast where there is continuity, homogeneity where there is variation. Yet the fact that these are observable practices clearly indicates that even knowledge of the neutral kind can be shown to be demonstrably constructed: from the sound up.

This focus on agency moves the analysis of phonemes and speech acts away from metapragmatic considerations and grounds it instead on linguistic behavior.

It is not just the "silent play of difference" between phonemes discussed by Dérida (1982: 88-90) that is of interest here, rather it is the behavior of speakers and listeners who experience phonemic discreteness by ignoring their experience of phonetic variation. While Dérida avoids the structural rigidity of classic, Saussurian semiology with his notion of sign as "deferred presence," he still presents the journey needed to bridge the hiatus between signifier and signified as internal to the sign itself. Whereas in this analysis the journey is undertaken by speakers and listeners in dialogic encounters.

In the same way, speech acts are not relevant here solely as theoretical models of the overt and covert levels of speech production. And this is not because we think speech acts may be untrustworthy, overgeneralized models, as has been argued by Silverstein and Rosaldo (Woolard 1998). Rather, they are useful as illustrations of linguistic *behavior*. Performatives do not lie, however "infelicitous" their condition. Speakers do.

Moreover, in Achino-Loeb's piece we begin to see the import of such analysis of silence for our experience of identity beyond that of sound. We begin to see why we should care about this; why it is essential to note that meaning depends on suppression of experience, starting from our experience of significance in sound. We see how such suppression is central in our experience and in our analysis of race as a category of identity. And race is singled out simply because it has been one of the categories of identity most resistant to deconstruction, as well as having been the category of identity most open to the exercise of raw power disguised as science, as Faye Harrison has argued (1998). However, implicit in this analysis is the understanding that *all* identity depends on suppression of experience and on selective analysis in order to survive.

Language ideology is even more transparent in practices that deny actual linguistic behavior in order to privilege preferred linguistic varieties. Susan Cook's piece picks up the issue of unobtrusive power exercised through linguistic manipulations and shows us how that works in the context of post-apartheid South Africa. She argues that preconceived, colonial ideas about language, ethnicity, nationhood, and their supposed consonance have determined language policy and ended up "erasing" the actual linguistic practices of people. What transpires from her research is a disjunction between the linguistic practices of black South Africans and the linguistic policies of those charged with education. The latter are reflected in the linguistic impositions found in schools, the former are reflected more closely in the media. While the actuality of linguistic practice is one of multilingualism and multidialectalism, the ideology is one that privileges standard Setswana—a dialect which is thought to be dying out, that is imposed as the "pure" or "clean" variety of Setswana; a dialect that most people "wouldn't be caught dead speaking." The result is that there is an attempt to silence the actual linguistic behavior of people by means of policies and their implementations in schools. That such erasure takes place within parameters that privilege non-European languages does not detract from its silencing effect. Rather, it points to the fruitfulness of language as vehicle for identity formation and of its manipulation for the attainment of power.

Cook's analysis also underlines the enduring quality of linguistic ideologies harnessed for social domination. That such concerns are products of a Colonial understanding equating language with territory gives us a sense of the enduring quality of categories of identity once enshrined in the collective consciousness. Habits of power are heavily indebted to practices of suppression of variation and privileging of sameness – whether such activities are conducted at the service of apartheid or anti-apartheid forces. In terms of practices of suppression, it matters less what the shape or ultimate purpose of the hegemony will be, than that it will be a hegemonic process. That those in governmental positions are more responsive to colonial philosophical assumptions than those in media positions, may tell us something about the enduring quality of habits of power, once bureaucratized, as Wolf has argued (1999). In all cases, the devolving of power requires sacrificing experience to the halter of unity of identity with its inherent homogenizing intents.

In sum, the first part of the book will take the reader by the hand through a detailed, deliberate articulation of how and why *silence* is the necessary precondition for the identification of meaning, for the privileging of some meanings, hence for the veiling of meaning which accompanies all ideological *programmes.*

False and True Consciousness: Silence in Ethnographic Experience

Various strands of this approach are given variable emphasis by different authors, yet the integrity of the argument is maintained throughout the book. The ethnographic pieces illustrate vividly the connection between meaning and power as it flows through the suppression of experience, hence they provide grounding for the inherence of silence discussed in part I. Silence is shown to be the overt political tool invoked as index of victimization by both the victimized (Sheriff) and the victimizers (Kingsolver); as inherent to the construction of an anthropological (subjects) reality, steeped as it is in serendipity (Barber, Fernandez); part and by-product of complex hegemonic systems fueled by globalized capital (Sider). These ethnographic accounts and analyses of the ethnographic enterprise raise significant questions regarding intentionality; just how free or inadvertent is the agency involved in this process. They plunge us headfirst into the fluidity of "silence" as domain of analysis; into some of the contradictions it raises; and, finally, into the murky waters of the culture versus ideology debate; of consciousness and its true versus false attributes.

At the other pole in the analysis of hegemony through linguistic imposition addressed by Cook, Ann Kingsolver's paper tackles the converse problem, namely how the language of victimization and resistance can be appropriated and usurped for purposes of self-affirmation through a process of othering she labels "strategic alterity."

In a comparative ethnography of semantic reversal, Kingsolver unravels the disingenuous linguistic twist that, holding silence as the ultimate evil, cloaked self-interest in free speech and allowed both Proposition 187—denying illegal aliens benefits or public services–and the confederate flag to "fly" in California and South Carolina, respectively. In Kingsolver's analysis the object of both was to identify and strengthen an idealized selfhood by racializing others, selectively, through what she calls "strategic alterity."

Much as with our perception of music or of phonemes, so the perception of Californians, in Kingsolver's analysis, has depended on the tacit reeling into oblivion of the complex demographic context and on drawing a binary opposition, white:Californian::Mexican:alien, intended to mark the boundaries of belonging as well as the condition of being alien. Contemporarily such activity has taken place by selective—and strategic—silencing of the complexity at hand. In her parallel with South Carolina and its confederate flag debacle, she also shows how such estrangement, intolerance, and discrimination are accepted and normalized by means of symbols that hold multiple referents, hence whose exclusive intents are cloaked under other guises. These symbols transmit their "hate speech"—which may otherwise not be protected under the law—in "complete silence" with a swift reversal of the terms of analysis, as critics are labeled "racist" for refusing to patronize white-owned establishments that fly the flag.

Paradoxically, free speech has been the contested crux of controversy; thereby bringing silence full circle from the condition of the oppressed to the political fig-leaf for the unabashed exercise of self-interest.

From a different vantage point, that of the observer, rather than the social actor, Barber presents us with the selective "elision" of crucial aspects in migrant women's experiences that allows observers/anthropologists to construe ideal types of "heroines" and "victims" and misconstrue fundamentally Philippine migration and its class implications. The culprit here is the theoretical positioning of analyses that overly rely on structural understandings of migration which have tended to be gendered. And the problem with gendering migrations, Barber argues, is that the actual experience of the women migrants is read in the key of what it does to or for women in their roles as nurturers; hence the heroine versus victim accounts.

Instead, women migrants are very proud of their role as economic supporters, even in the face of the actual hardships they encounter. While pushed by structural forces, these women have more options than a strictly victimized analysis would grant them and their subjective class experiences are centered around the issue of dignity they derive from their sense of discharged duty. If we should redress some of these silences and give voice to the realities muted by our predetermined and skewed choice of relevance, we would see that there are strong class implications to women's migration, in the sending and receiving countries.

Therefore, the model of silence as inherent to the construction of specific identities discussed in part I of the book holds sway here. The suggestion is that the very activity of identity formation is an analytic practice, whether undertaken by outsiders or insiders—one that involves delineating boundaries of relevance and salience; which boundaries exclude even as they include. In the case of Philippine women, they exclude their lived experiences in favor of predetermined, overly theorized structural positioning as family supporters and nurturers. This structural positioning is not false: women do nurture their families via remittances. Rather, such gender-role focused analyses are partial. They don't include the women's agency in the adoption and alteration of class belonging. Yet these very practices may be at the heart of their class consciousness.

In Kingsolver and Barber, then, we begin to see the outlines of a controversy regarding the import and degree of consciousness in agency. In both cases it is clear that identity is not a given and that the agency involved in its delineation is identifiable either in the social actors themselves (Kingsolver) or in the observer (Barber). Further, the agency can be advertent and political (Kingsolver) or inadvertent and naïve (Barber). The important issue is that in order to understand the degree of authenticity of identity we need to unpack the contexts that produced it, veiled as they are by multiple layers of the unsaid or of the purposely muted.

The play between false and true consciousness is brought out even more starkly in Sheriff's analysis of racism in Brazil where she grapples with the incongruence between an inequitable social system where privileges bestowed and withheld run along racial lines and, until fairly recently, the dearth of discussion surrounding race and racism in Brazil, bathed as it has been in the ideology of "democracia racial." Her object is to show how silence can be both an indispensable means for the success of hegemonic enterprises and an adaptive tool when truth-telling is either impolitic or impossible.

While "cultural censorship" regarding racism does exist and affects unobtrusively even that which is untouched by overt domination, such cultural censorship is not complete. Sheriff shows us that the existence of racial hierarchy is both clear in the mind of her informants and evidenced in their everyday unguarded speech. She also shows us how the veiling capacity of such censorship affects people differently, depending on their position in the racial hierarchy. Accordingly, black Brazilians know of its importance, ubiquity, and wide-ranging effects, yet they keep silent for reasons of "practicality," in recognition of their effective powerlessness in redressing it. While their white neighbors swallow the ideology of "democracia racial," hook, line, and sinker. If there is any false consciousness in that matter, it affects whites only, as the cultural censorship is successful in cushioning their class position with an elaborate justification of race as unimportant in Brazilian social life.

Silence, as we have seen, works precisely because it allows us to believe that the unspoken is nonexistent. Yet, as we have also seen, the unspoken does not disappear; rather it is glossed differently. For black Brazilians subject to the irresistible sway of cultural censorship veiling the existence of racial hierarchy, the unspoken presence of racism surfaces in the powerful image of the "Escrava Anastácia," the slave with black skin and blue eyes who was literally muzzled by her lecherous owner and who died from the treatment. Her figure and the common understandings of its iconic import are clear indications of black Brazilians' acknowledgement of the existence of racism, of its destructiveness, and of the silence under which it has been wrapped. Therefore, the motivational forces underlying the easy, unproblematic acceptance of the ideology regarding race are deeply marked by self-interest.

This part of the book, then, illuminates in fuller ethnographic narrative the journey that silence undertakes in its role as currency of power, which we earlier examined in its perceptual and linguistic dimensions. It shows how the construction of identity boundaries—whether undertaken by social actors or observers—is embedded in the suppression of variation and complexity; how agency—however inadvertent—is central to such construction and at the service of hegemonic forces of domination and resistance that skew this or that aspect of signification to attain their goals.

Such approaches point to the precariousness of a false consciousness analysis that ignores the incidence and degree of agency involved in the very process of identity formation through the selective perception of significance we already saw operative in the linguistic examples. At the same time, they point to the elements of convergence in the modernist and postmodernist perspectives.

The understanding that knowledge is partial, experience is illusory, and both are manipulable is at the heart of the "depth model" (Jameson 1991:12) of reality that, particularly in its Marxian permutations, has been the source for the understanding of ideology as mystification, curable only through changed contexts (Jameson 1981). It is also the refrain in the constructionist approach to the social, which has sowed doubt on the very possibility of its analysis (Clifford 1986). The depth model discussed by Jameson, particularly the dialectical model based on the interplay between essence and appearance and the Freudian model of repression, posits that the deep aspect of reality can be penetrated by specialists, be they philosophers, organic intellectuals, or psychoanalysts. While the constructionist approach critiques this very trust in the penetrability of reality which, when perceived by observers, is fictive by definition.

Hence, one consensus underlying these divergent approaches is that a full vision of reality is largely unavailable, since its depth dimensions open it only to the understanding of the few, or that it is untrustworthy because fabricated out of whole cloth. In either case, the veiling and fabrication are due to identifiable self-interests that skew the attention of most onlookers and participants alike. Our analysis of silence shows that such agency is inherent to the meaning construction process, as elements of potential significance depend on active suppression of experience in order to be identified. Therefore, the very experience of depth is created by the process of suppression *and* the perception of reality is forged in the privileging of salience.

This means that both modernist and postmodernist approaches are onto something.

For the *depth* is there, not a myth as Lacan may argue (Borch-Jacobsen 1991). Yet such depth is not an a-priori attribute of structure, as may be argued in classic Saussurian semiotics with the signifier/signified polarity of signs (Saussure 1968). Nor is depth inherently beyond the reach of apprehension, as may be argued in classic Marxist analyses of *value* underneath the exchange value of commodities (Marx 1976). Rather, depth is constituted in lived practices of silence: more akin to *habitus* (Bourdieu 1977) than to essence. Similarly, knowledge is indeed manipulated, but the manipulability of knowledge begins in the first instances of identification, when the experience of variation is ignored in favor of agreed-upon relevance, rather than starts at the overt manipulation of ideas. In fact, it is at this primary level of selective assigning of salience that ideological manipulations are at their most elusive. For they tend to disappear behind concerns with culture and its parameters, as they do in the *connectionist model* endeavoring to explain precisely the avenues for the privileging of salience in shared schemas (Strauss and Quinn 1997).

Our theoretical approach to silence is less concerned with the viability of the culture concept giving impetus to current schema theory than it is focused on identifying *agency* in the selectivity and suppression attending the internalization of schemas. Shared meanings may well proceed from the intersection of internalized schemas, but the process is not serendipitous; intentions play a large role even in the successful communication of speech. Intentions are even more openly causative in systems of economic and political inequality. What begs analysis are the foci of self-interest that determine the parameters of each context.

Ideas and power "intermesh" (Wolf 1999:1) *before* they are part of ideological systems. The perception and manipulation of significance are, in fact, mutually generative, according to this analysis, as we have seen in the example of specific identities, their endurance, and the political self-interests that shaped and continue to rely on them. Even the prototype of analyses of mystification, the fetishism of commodities engaged by Marx (1976), leads to such understanding when examined dispassionately. For commodities are fetishized precisely because there is a recognition, below the level of consciousness though it might be, that they stand for more then their exchange value; that they embody social labor; even as the mode of production giving rise to the conditions for such fetishism continues to thrive from it.

The road to overt ideological domination rests on a bedrock of silence running through different layers of suppression that bend perspective at the service of contextual cohesiveness; where the parameters of the context are not haphazard, but rest on the groove of various self-interests ranging from linguistic continuity to economic and political hegemony. These layers of suppression begin at selective perception of significance and end in the consensus that, Gramsci (1971) taught us, is the necessary condition for the effective wielding of power. Hence a large dimension of the consensus is based on silence.

The Plight of the Observer

Finally, the volume takes up the issue of ethnographic work, its goal, and how it is marred by both the intentions of the ethnographer and the intentions of the observed, the needs of the ethnographic enterprise and the inherent complexity of the context. In many of the contributions, as we have seen, the eye of the observer lurks beneath concerns with arbitrariness in the construction of identity (Achino-Loeb, Cook, Kingsolver) and with authenticity in the embracing and in the inscription of identity (Sheriff, Barber, Kingsolver).

It is the observer's own baggage of knowledge and intentions that is responsible for the partial way in which identity boundaries reflect the experience of those so identified. As observers, we actively participate in the construction of our objects of observation: in part, because the questions we ask, the areas we highlight, the selective recognition of salience direct the spotlight to some aspects of experience and not others, thereby permitting the recognition of only some elements of significance (Beeman, Achino-Loeb, Fernandez); in part, because the baggage of knowledge we bring to the task or the intentions that direct our search skews the inherently partial nature of the knowability of things in one direction or another—thereby erasing, eliding, muting or generally suppressing all others (Achino-Loeb, Cook, Kingsolver, Barber, Sheriff, Sider).

The last two chapters pointedly focus on the limits of the ethnographic enterprise (Fernandez) and on the political responsibility of ethnographers (Sider). The crux of Sider's contribution is to present us with the inevitability of mystification—given the social transformations wrought by a globalized economy constantly churning and spewing off workers as the labor of different cohorts loses or gains value—as well as to argue the need to overcome it. Sider suggests that anthropology's impotence in describing the localized effects of such changes is due to its attachment to "bankrupt" concepts that unjustifiably privilege a theorized cohesiveness –of culture, of society, of kin, etc.—when such concepts only describe the experience of a restricted core of participants in the new economy, while the majority are simply caught in its chaos. The observer's lens should be aimed at the *ruptures* produced by this new economy—ruptures in the social fabric and ruptures of vision—that insulate local people from a clear understanding of their situation.

In Sider we encounter several levels of suppression affecting both social actors and observers. On the one hand there is an active veiling of reality taking place at the structural level of power. On the other hand, the intimation is that such veiling is unavoidable, since the walls of silence are erected by whirlwind changes that use up people as resources limiting their knowledge in the process. And observers are charged with the Gramscian role of organic intellectuals who foster change by unveiling or bridging those ruptures. Hence analytic integrity is coterminous with political engagement in this perspective.

Fernandez brings the analysis back to the inevitability of silence that eased in our initial argument: suppression is unavoidable because it is simply not possible to capture all and knowledge is partial by definition. Whereas Sider gives voice to the pathos of observers vainly tearing at veils of mystification with inappropriate tools, Fernandez takes us full circle to the epistemological angst attending any awareness of the inherence of silence; to the practical impossibility of extracting ourselves from relationality enough to erase the constant questioning regarding the various "what ifs"—what if we had included that voice, that opinion… . He gives voice to the privileging imperative that accompanies the ethnographic enterprise, echoing earlier arguments (Beeman, Achino-Loeb), and to the inevitable bias attending any ethnographic second person account, evoking many a deconstructionist voice (Clifford and Marcus, eds. 1986); a bias stemming from the selectivity involved in the choice of sources deemed relevant.

At the end of the day, literally in the ethnographer's case, we record those voices we trust; voices that became our evidence of a reality we have constructed in the process of selecting "informants," sequences of events we thrust onto memory, tape-recorders or the written page. His quote of Frankel is worth reprinting here.

> *Our knowledge of the "really real" is mediated by fallible perceptions and imperfect reason. Human knowledge of reality can never be either complete or certain, therefore; instead it involves selective interpretations of whatever may actually exist. Thus, although we may not construct the world, we have no choice but to construe it.* (15)

The rest of his chapter turns this dictum on its head and delineates the parameters of absences he estimates present in his work. For here too, that which is silenced does not disappear but lives on in *head notes* that accompany our muffled memories of the past.

Part III of the book, then, revisits the duality of concerns regarding silence and its import present throughout; namely, the arbitrariness underlying the choice of salience in assigning significance and the inherent manipulability of the process. Hence, agency looms beneath these analyses, as well. Agency accompanies the choice of salient voices, as we have seen. Agency is even more overt in analyses that privilege the position of the observer as organic intellectual who holds a key to knowledge unavailable to the masses.

What is clear from all these analyses is that we *can* look at silence. Contrary to poststructuralist approaches characterized by a sense of the "intractable" in human experience (Dillon 2000), our argument is that the intractable itself is constructed. Silence is our parallel to the intractable; that which resists representation but is not beyond it. The walls of silence are never impermeable. If we want to understand how power works, we must look at the interstitial spaces where meaning is ambiguous; the spaces beyond the margins of meaning, where significance is up for grabs, but is there nevertheless and involved in a neverending chase with this or that signifier. We must look at the spaces of withheld judgment, of deferred opinion, of incipient if timid understanding just as much as we look at the well-defined spaces of prohibition, of censorship, of squelching of perspective. For this is the way in which power works unobtrusively.

Therefore this book stands at the cusp of the divide between modernist and postmodernist understandings of meaning, identity, and power. On the one hand, many of the analyses give voice to important tonalities in the Marxist tradition, according to which a major element of the effectiveness of power is one of mystification undertaken in direct or indirect support of economic and political hegemony. On the other hand, such mystification is seen in epistemological terms as the unavoidable effect of identity formation, which in turn is seen as the necessary prerequisite for the perception of meaning and the limits it inheres.

Recognizing the ideological foundation of all knowledge moves the analysis away from true versus false knowledge and toward the *contexts* that make the privileging of specific salience and formation of identity desirable or advantageous; which contexts encompass the careful screening of the self-interests involved in even the more benign identification of salience from both the insider and outsider perspectives.

Debates that pit the position of the observer in direct contrast to that of the social actor have been burdened by controversies regarding the outer reaches of the *emic / etic* referents (Goodenough 2002) and poorly served by the assumption that reflexivity equals unshackled subjectivity operating beyond the analytic rules that govern other—objectivist-knowledge (Salzman 2002). These positional debates are rendered moot by the recognition that both the outsider and insider perspectives must undergo the process of selectivity/suppression that undergirds the perception of any and all significance as instances of identity. As knowledge, the emic is no more authentic or unburdened by the pull of perspective than the etic, even at its most reflexive. At the same time, the emic is not beyond analysis. Rather, it is as subject to analysis as the contexts that produced it are transparent.

This focus on silence with its privileging of the *context* is an invitation to frame our analyses within parameters rendered appropriate by our questions of research, rather than by the meta-narrative *du jour.* For any meta-narrative can be "good to think and good for thinking," in Godelier's happy phrasing (2000: 310).

As domain of analysis, *silence* brings transparency to the practice-based logic that sustains fixing identity along predictable boundaries. Through its analysis the outlines of habits of power surface in multiple guises of empowerment, domination, or resistance on the heels of variations in self-interests. For, in silence, the manifest is not allowed to erase the latent; and it is in latency that the possibility for change persists; echoing shifting contexts; open to a discerning ear.

References Cited

Austin, John L. 1962 *How to Do Things with Words.* Oxford: Oxford University Press.

Basso, Keith. 1970. "To Give Up on Words: Silence in Western Apache Culture." In *Language and Social Context.* Pier Paolo Giglioli, ed. Pp.67-86. New York: Penguin Books.

Beckett, Samuel. *Waiting for Godot.* New York: Grove Press.

Borch-Jacobsen, Mikkel. 1991. *Lacan: The Absolute Master.* Douglas Brick, trans. Stanford: Stanford University Press.

Bourdieu, Pierre. 1977. *Outline of a Theory of Practice.* Cambridge: Cambridge University Press.

Cardinal, Agnes. 2000. "Quest in a Cupboard." In *Secret Spaces, Forbidden Places; Rethinking Culture.* New York: Berghan Books.

Clifford, James. 1986. "Introduction: Partial Truths." In *Writing Culture: The Politics and Poetics of Ethnography.* James Clifford and George E. Marcus, eds.,1-26. Berkeley: University of California Press.

Clifford, James and George E. Marcus, eds. 1986. *Writing Culture: The Politics and Poetics of Ethnography.* Berkeley: University of California Press.

Dérida, Jacques. 1982. *Margins of Philosophy.* Chicago: University of Chicago Press.

Dillon, Michael. 2000. "Poststructuralism, Complexity and Poetics." In *Theory, Culture and Society*, 17 (5): 1-26.

Frankel, Barbara. 1981. *Two Roshomon Effects and the Puzzled Ethnographer: On the Epistemology of Listening to Different Voices,* unpublished manuscript. 65 pgs.

Fuss, Diana. 1989. *Essentially Speaking.* New York: Routledge.

Godelier, Maurice. 2000. "Is Social Anthropology Still Worth the Trouble? A Response to Some Echoes from America." In *Ethnos,* 65(3): 301-316.

Goodenough, Ward H. 2002. "Anthropology in the 20th Century and Beyond." *American Anthropologist* 104(2): 423-440.

Gordon, Colin, ed. 1972. *Power/Knowledge: Selected Interviews & Other Writings 1972-1977 by Michel Foucault.* New York: Pantheon Books.

Gramsci, Antonio. 1971. "Il Moderno Principe: Notarelle sulla Politica del Macchiavelli." In *Gramsci: Scritti Politici.* Paolo Spriano, ed.745-803. Roma: Editori Riuniti.

Harrison, Faye V. 1998. "Introduction: Expanding the Discourse on Race." *American Anthropologist* 100(3): 609-631.

Hoy, David Couzens. 1986. "Introduction." In *Foucault: A Critical Reader.* David Couzens Hoy, ed.: 1-25. Oxford and Cambridge, Mass: Blackwell Publishers, Ltd.

Jameson, Fredric. 1981. *The Political Unconscious: Narrative as a Socially Symbolic Act.* Ithaca, New York: Cornell, University Press.

_____ 1991. *Postmodernism, or, the Cultural Logic of Late Capitalism.* Durham, N. C.: Duke University Press.

Lukacs, Georg. 1968. *History and Class Consciousness.* Cambridge: M.I.T. Press.

Marx, Karl. 1976. *Capital* (Volume One, Chapter 1: The Commodity). New York: Vintage Books.

Rinpoche, Sogyal. 1993. *The Tibetan Book of Living and Dying.* San Francisco: Harper.

Salzman, Philip Carl. 2002. "On Riflexivity." *American Anthropologist* 104(3): 805-813.

Saussure, Ferdinand de. [1916]1968. *Cours de Linguistique Generale.* Gottingen: Hubert & Co.

Sheriff, Robin. 2000. "Exposing Silence as Cultural Censorship: A Brazilian Case." *American Anthropologist* 102(1): 3-28.

Strauss, Claudia and Naomi Quinn. 1997. *A Cognitive Theory of Cultural Meaning.* Cambridge: Cambridge University Press.

Tannen, Deborah and Muriel Saville Troike, eds. 1985. *Perspectives on Silence.* Norwood, N.J.: Ablex Publishing.

Wolf, Eric R. 1999. *Envisioning Power: Ideologies of Dominance and Crisis.* Berkeley: University of California Press.

_____ 2001. "Facing Power: Old Insights, New Questions." In *Pathways of Power: Building an Anthropology of the Modern World* (with Sydel Silverman). Berkeley: University of California Press.

Woolard, Kathryn A. 1997. "Introduction: Language Ideology as a Field of Inquiry." In *Language Ideologies: Practice and Theory.* Bambi B. Schieffelin, Kathryn A. Woolard, & Paul V. Kroskrity, eds.: 3-47. New York: Oxford University Press.

PART I

Silence, Context, and Categories of Identity

Chapter 1

Silence in Music

William O. Beeman

The music I like best is the music we make when there is no music
– John Cage (1961)

Music is beautiful when it stops
– Stefan Zweig (librettist, from Richard Strauss' *Die Schweigsame Frau*)

Pauses and holds are music
– Kurt Adler (1971)

Introduction

Several years ago, I came to San Francisco to record a new, original piece of music written by a California composer. As I read through the music for the first time, I realized that there was something drastically wrong with the piece. It had no rests. Beside posing a practical problem for a singer—there was no place to breathe—there was a more serious musical problem. After a while it was impossible to hear the piece. Its elements were buried in the overall wall of continuous sound.

Working with the composer, I was able to create a performable piece of music by introducing pauses and rests. This exercise taught me quite a bit about the function of silence in music, and has caused me to speculate about the nature of silence altogether in more generalized forms of communication.

This essay consists of several sections in which I talk about silence as a function of information in figure-ground relationships, silence as a boundary function and silence as a function of turn-taking in music. Finally I will discuss John Cage's revolutionary work, *4'33"* and its significance for a broader consideration of cultural phenomena similar to that of the question of silence vs. non-silence.

First, however, I must establish a central fact: *silence is not an acoustic phenomenon: it is a cultural construct.*

Silence as a Cultural Construct

There is no such thing in human life as an absence of sound except for those for whom the absence of sound is part of the steady state of existence, because they are profoundly deaf. Arguably, silence is also not a part of the universe of the deaf, because they have no sound environment with which to contrast it.

In short: silence as a phenomenon can be defined only in contrast to sound, moreover, it is established in contrast to *particular*, culturally designated sound. Therefore, silence is *de-facto* a type of sound, contrasted with other types of sound. It is the element of contrast that is important, and this contrast is likewise a construction.

As will be seen below, one cannot use any "essentialist" definition to delineate silence as, for example, the absence of sound, since nothing we can identify as silence lacks sound. It could possibly be thought of as the absence of purposefully constructed sound, but in music, as well as in speech—two areas where silence plays a substantial role, those episodes where the vibration of the air that we identify as sound is lacking, are also constructed.

Moreover, the cessation of purposefully constructed vibrating air allows literally "the sounds of silence" to be heard. These "sounds of silence" are namely, the ambient environmental vibrations not intended by the musician or the speaker of language.

This was the central intellectual point raised by John Cage in his famous composition *4'33"*, arguably one of the most influential artistic statements in the history of music. I will return to a discussion of this work later. However, let it suffice to say that one of Cage's aims in the piece was to demonstrate to an audience that distinguishing music from silence is a problem of cognitive framing. In the absence of specific sounds designated as music, the ambient sound in the performance environment becomes the acoustic content of the work—in essence that which audience members were disposed to designate as "silence" is reframed as "sound."

Silence as Information

Since Shannon and Weaver (1949) we have understood information to be the inverse of probability. This is to say, information content increases as an inverse function of probability. In lay terms, the less probable something is, the more information it carries.

The Shannon and Weaver notion of information is closely tied to the Gestalt psychology notion of *figure* and *ground*. The "ground" is the disattended phenomenon against which the "figure" is presented and stands out. In art, the "ground" is the background canvas and frame upon which the artistic product is displayed. Great artists from time immemorial have played with this relationship unceasingly. Most notably Escher, in whose eye-popping images, the figure and ground are continually reversed.

Figure 1.1: Escher—Woodcut II, Strip 3

In Woodcut II, Strip 3, one sees the black "ground" at the left of the strip gradually become more elaborate as a repeated pattern, emerging as the "figure" on the right. Similarly the white "figure" at the left gradually loses detail as it repeats toward the right, eventually becoming the "ground" for the black figures[1].

The acoustic phenomenon we label as "silence" is fascinating in this regard. In fact, it has a dual function both as high-information content and as low-information content in music. This is not a paradox. Shannon and Weaver's definition depends on context. Specifically recognized music has high information content *vis-à-vis* the ambient sound that proceeds and follows it. This ambient sound is then designated as *silence* and has low information content, because it represents the steady state "ground" against which music becomes a "figure."

By contrast, a pause or a rest in the course of music has high information content because it becomes a "figure" against the "ground" of the constant musical expression. There are some poignant examples in

music—perhaps the most familiar being the "grand pause" at the end of the "Halleluja Chorus" from Handel's *Messiah,* seen in the following example in the third measure from the end. In practice, the two beat rest is frequently lengthened considerably. The drama in this pause is so great that unsuspecting audience members, thinking that the piece has ended, will frequently begin to applaud during the "silence." This is a "roll one's eyes" moment for the musicians and chorus in silent contemplation of the lack of sophistication of the audience. Such examples are memorable, because they are somewhat rare.

Figure 1.2: Example 1—Halleluja Chorus

A second example will demonstrate how unexpected such events are in Schubert's famous song *Du bist die Ruh.*

One sees Schubert indicating a full measure pause of both instrumental and vocal sound in the song, not once, but twice (indicated in the final measure of the next to the last stave, and the fourth from the last stave). The dramatic hiatus separates a forte crescendo from a pianissimo reply. The contrast between the two dynamics might not be so poignant without the measure of rest.

In both cases, the pause exists to emphasize the drama of the preceding material, and to set up a sharp contrast with the following material: in the Händel example, a sharp change in tempo and a final, definitive cadence;

Figure 1.3: Example 2—Du bist die Ruh

in the Schubert case, a sharp dynamic change, a shift of tonal center and a contrast in the phrasing.

The pause can also be used as a means of allowing a musical phrase to resonate and reverberate before the initiation of a new phrase as in this example from Persian classical music.

Figure 1.4: Example 3—Persian classical music—Daramad of Shur

The example above is in the "dastgah" or mode of Shur (after Farhat 1990). Persian music is organized into groups of small melodic units called "gusheh." In classical performance tradition, the small melodic units are chosen and played by the performer in improvisatory form. The example above is the "Daramad" (Introduction)—the first piece in Shur. One section of the traditional classical music performance is non-metered. The rests indicated in this transcription are merely advisory. In practice, the performer pauses at the end of each phrase to allow the instrument he or she is playing to echo the final notes of the phrase. This ambient echo is part of the aesthetics of the performance.

Silence as Boundary

Music, such as the Persian example above, consists of phrases and statements much like in human discourse. Except for certain minimalist works, such as seen in the works of composer Phillip Glass, these phrases are separated from each other by spates of silence. In this manner, silence serves to mark boundaries between the basic segmental units of music.

The principal boundary is that which marks the beginning and the end of a piece of music. The secondary boundaries mark sections within a musical work, such as the movements of a symphony or the pauses between songs in a song cycle. Audience conventions in the presentation of live music require that the integrity of a whole work, such as a concerto, symphony, song cycle, or section of a recital not be broken by applause, but be sanctified by silence. Tertiary boundaries mark breaks in musical statements. Musical analysis generally starts by showing how these boundaries operate.

We don't need to listen to a whole symphony or song cycle to demonstrate the primary and secondary boundary mechanisms, but tertiary phrases are easily illustrated in solo instrument works such as the partitas for violin and cello by Bach. These works are fascinating, because in them Bach does *not* indicate rests or pauses. Nevertheless, they illustrate perfectly the concept of *relative* volume as an interpretative mechanism. They must be phrased in order to be comprehensible to the listener. Simply giving every note equal value destroys the figure-ground relationship in the music, and makes it unhearable.

In the next example, the lowest note in every figure of four notes, the low G is de-emphasized. In effect the low G becomes the "silence" that separates each phrase. It is the tonic note of the harmony, and thus is present throughout the piece as an harmonic "anchor." It becomes the ground against which the harmonies of the piece develop.

Figure 1.5: Example 4—Bach cello suite #1—Prelude in G major

Silence as Turn Taking

Nothing can illustrate the concept of "relative silence" better than contrapuntal forms in music. In contrapuntal music, instruments and voices, or multiple voices engage in "conversation" during the course of a work. Musical statements are followed by silence in which the other instrument or instruments produce a response or an extension of the original. An instrumental duet usually plays on this important function. Schumann uses this feature extensively in his justifiably famous songs, as in the example below "Im Wonderschönen Monat Mai.

Figure 1.6: Example 5—Schumann-Im Wonderschönen Monat Mai

In this song the piano and voice are in equal collaboration. The piano figure in the beginning with the rising arpeggios becomes the "ground"

against which the vocal line is displayed. The voice pauses, as indicated by the rests indicated in boxes in example 5, to allow the piano once again to emerge as figure against the ground of the vocal pause. This turn-taking converges in concerted form as the two musical voices overlap in harmony.

This is seen in particular in jazz idioms where every instrumentalist usually gets a turn to "take the floor" as in face-to-face conversation. Thus the individual "voices" in music (which can be instrumental) are seen to adopt silence vis-à-vis the other voices as music proceeds. In a typical performance by a jazz ensemble, each instrument gets an opportunity to "riff," against the ground of an accompaniment, usually by a bass instrument playing minimal rhythms and chords.

4'33"

No discussion of silence in music would be complete without a discussion of John Cage's *4'33"*. I provide a brief description of the piece by Larry J. Solomon paraphrasing Calvin Tomkins, who witnessed the piece for those who are unfamiliar with it.

> The piece lasts for four minutes and thirty-three seconds in which the performer plays nothing … .It was first performed by the young pianist David Tudor at Woodstock, New York on August 29, 1952. Tudor placed the hand-written score, which was in convential notation with blank measures, on the piano and sat motionless as he used a stopwatch to measure the time of each movement. The score indicated three silent movements, each of a different length, but when added together totalled four minutes and thirty-three seconds [30", 2'23", 1'40"]. Tudor signaled its commencement by lowering the keyboard lid of the piano. The sound of the wind in the trees entered the first movement. After thirty seconds of no action, he raised the lid to signal the end of the first movement. It was then lowered for the second movement, during which raindrops pattered on the roof. The score was in several pages, so he turned the pages as time passed, yet played nothing at all. The keyboard lid was raised and lowered again for the final movement, during which the audience whispered and muttered (Solomon 1998: 1 citing Tomkins 1965).

Although designated as a "silent piece," this is a misnomer. Cage was quite clear in his belief that there was no such thing as silence. After having visited an anechoic chamber at Harvard and having experienced a low and a high tone, he was informed that the low tone was his heartbeat, and the high tone his circulation system. His conclusion was "Try as we may to make a silence, we cannot. One need not fear for the future of music (Cage 1961: 8). 4'33" was also not an isolated work, but was rather an extension of Cage's random compositional technique, evolved starting with his association with Arnold Schoenberg (Solomon 1998: 4).

Cage's intellectual point in 4'33" has been interpreted variously as indicating that ambient sound *is* music, that ambient sound *is a part* of music. Cage himself was clear that he was trying to redefine the relationship between music, the *figure* and everyday life, the *ground* against which music is played:

> I'm trying to find a way to make music that does not depend on time. ... [It's] nothing but the continuation of one's daily work. ... What the piece is trying to say is that everything we do is music, or can become music (Cage in Kostelanetz 1988: 69-70).

Composer and Musician Larry Solomon takes the performance of 4' 33" very seriously. The performance conditions mark the absence of all but ambient sound as "framed" in an artistic sense. By providing a beginning, ending and specific transitional structures, the ambient sound—the "silence" of 4'33" emerges as the artistic figure of the piece. Solomon recommends the following performance practices to give the piece its full presentational framing:

Performance Recommendations

- Avoid all distracting, extraneous actions, choreography, intentional sounds, etc., that could detract from focusing attention upon the environmental, unintentional sounds.
- The performers' demeanor and part in the music should be passive, static, and reserved, yet serious, focused, attentive, and respectful.
- Either the prescribed timings of the *Kremen Edition* should be used or timings should be constructed for three movements using chance operations. These need not total 4'33". I do not recommend the spurious timings of the *Tacet Editions.*
- A score should be used, preferably the *Kremen Edition*, with page turns (but not a separate page-turner).
- A stopwatch should be used to keep track of the movement lengths.

- Some simple, non-obtrusive action should be taken to mark the separate movements. For example, a performer could display three large cards on a music stand, each of which would announce the movement number.
- The three separate movements, with their respective timings, should be listed in the printed program.
- *4'33"* is not a piano piece, but a piece for **any** instrument or instruments. Its reputation as strictly a piano piece needs to be overcome by more performances on other instruments. (Solomon 1998)

Solomon's last point was illustrated in a performance at Brown University in 2003 when 4'33" was premiered in a version for Chinese gong. The event was quasi-whimsical in its intent, but nonetheless effective as an artistic statement.

Silence, Music and Anthropology

Cage brings the structures of silence in music into high relief by collapsing the functions of silence.

1) The social and cultural distinction between sound and silence is immediately brought into clear relief in this piece, and in Cage's many discussions of it (e.g. Cage 1961).
2) The informational distinctions between figure and ground are eliminated. As the audience becomes aware that the ground (the "silence") *is* the figure, it acquires high information content.
3) The boundary between performance and non-performance is blurred. Although there are visual cues in 4'33" that signal the beginning and end of the piece, the audience is uncertain about the beginning of the work. They come to understand it gradually.
4) Finally, the contrapuntal nature of silence is also brought into play in a very dramatic manner. With no distinct "voices" everything in the world is in counterpoint with everything else. Making an "audience" aware of this begins to depart from the world of art, and enter the world of philosophy or religion. This is not accidental. Cage's work was deeply inspired by such considerations, particularly as they are reflected in Asian religious disciplines.

It is my hope that anthropologists will be able to see the question of silence vs. non-silence as an important distinction extensible into other areas of cultural life. What is ritual vs. non-ritual? What is art vs. non-art? What is communication vs. non-communication (cf. Basso 1970, Hanks 1996: 2-3, 121-122)? All of these problems involve the same questions of social/cultural definition, figure-ground informational distinctions, boundary problems, and "cultural counterpoint" in the form of concerted alternation and turn taking in human life.

In particular, it should be clear that just as the notion of silence is ephemeral—being in reality a culturally defined category of sound—so are "silences," "absences," and "inactions" in other aspects of human life mere appearances. They are likewise categorizations of sound, presence and action.

One example in ritual is the silent prayer, or moment of silence that often accompanies expressions of respect. As a pause in the activity of a meeting or assembly, it raises the "silence" to the level of figure, and the normal activity of the gathering recedes to become the ground against which it is presented.

In the quest for universal human cognitive and behavioral trends, anthropologists could do far worse than to look to these basic structures of music for a useful set of analogies for other cultural structures in which the interplay of culturally defined figure and ground play a principal role.

Notes

1. Reuven Tsur gives many more examples, and in particular in a series of on-line papers, provides many interesting examples from music, literature and art of the interplay of figure and ground. (See Tsur 1998) See also his larger work in book form *Toward a Theory of Cognitive Poetics* (1992).

References cited:

Adler, Kurt. 1971. *The Art of Accompanying and Coaching*, Corr. edition. New York: Da Capo Press.

Basso, Keith 1970. *To Give Up on Words: Silence in Western Apache Culture.* Southwestern Journal of Anthropology 26: 213-30.

Cage, John 1961. *Silence.* Middletown, CT: Wesleyan University Press.

Farhat, Hormoz 1990. *The Dastgāh Concept in Persian Music.* Cambridge: Cambridge University Press.

Hanks, William F. 1996. *Language and Communicative Practices.* Boulder, CO: Westview Press.

Kostelanetz, Richard 1988. *Conversing with Cage.* New York: Limelight

Reisman, Karl 1974. "Contrapuntal Conversations in an Antiguan Village". In *Explorations in the Ethnography of Speaking.* Richard Bauman and Joel Sherzer, Eds., Pp. 110-124. Cambridge: Cambridge University Press.

Shannon, Claude E. and Warren Weaver. 1949. *The Mathematical Theory of Communication.* Urbana, Ill.: University of Illinois Press.

Solomon, Larry J. 1998. *The Sounds of Silence: John Cage and 4'33".*

Tomkins, Calvin 1965. *The Bride & The Bachelors.* New York: Penguin/Viking.

Tsur, Reuven 1992. *Toward a Theory of Cognitive Poetics.* Amsterdam: Elsevier (North Holland) Science Publishers.

_____ 1998. "Metaphor and Figure-Ground Relationship: Comparisons from Poetry, Music, and the Visual Arts." On-line publication. <http://www.tau.ac.il/~tsurxx/Figure-ground+sound.html>

CHAPTER 2

SILENCE AND THE IMPERATIVES OF IDENTITY

Maria-Luisa Achino-Loeb

The object of this chapter will be to explore the role of silence in the delineation and in the experience of identity by tracing its inherence to the perception of meaning in language. I will hold that the dimensions of silence on which we depend in order to perceive significance in sound and in speech constitute a system of habitual practices that in turn provide the ground for our—purportedly innate—categorical experience of identity.

The main thrust of this argument rests on the assumption that identity is not a condition, rather it is an activity which ultimately depends on silence for its successful realization. And the agency implicated in identity is manifest in the characteristics that accompany its very formation and maintenance, namely,

- arbitrariness in the delineation of boundaries;
- selectivity in the choice of salience among its constitutive elements;
- suppression of experience that does not conform with such selection;
- hence inherent openness to manipulations at the service of self-interest.

Much of this understanding is not new, as it is part and parcel of the critique of essentialist positions. What will be underlined here is the *silence* inherent to the process of identity formation. For it is this dimension of identity that allows the most egregious, yet subtle workings of agency, skewing reality at the service of self-interest. Hence it is the locus where *power* can take root even before the self-interest involved becomes apparent: a major concern of this book. In order to understand how identity becomes foundational and how "foundational categories of identity"[1] become naturalized, we need to understand the "cultural logic" that underlies them, as Faye Harrison has argued (1998). To do that, we must look at silence, for, as has been noted, "the creation of the conceptual order is also, constitutively, the suppression of aspects of reality" (Valeri in Wolf 2001: 395).

The contention here will be that silence is the concept we need in order to trust that our categories of experience *are* discrete, as opposed to arbitrary bindings of fluidity.

Hence the final object of this chapter will be to operationalize the notion of *silence* as the framework for the internalizing, naturalizing and, therefore, for the essentializing of identity.

Of Flux and Salience

The sense that we are at the mercy of a flux of stimuli, awaiting organization to acquire significance is not new, it is in fact at the heart of linguistic relativity (Kay 1999). The point has always been *how* such organization takes place; how do we habitually form "classes of classes"(Ervin-Tripp 1999). For whether such capacity is product of quantitative, as opposed to qualitative uniqueness in our evolutionary path (Gibson 1999), the end result has been precisely the very skill humans employ to appraise stimuli in terms of identifiable, if contingent, categories (Schumann 1999). Goodenough is most overt about the import of such appraisal skill: "For a sensory input to have value as a stimulus with an associated learned response, it must be perceived as an instance or member of a categorical set" (1999: 24).

Hence the experience of salience is both central to the discreteness of sensory input and marked by contrast. Yet, such contrast is not always self-evident, as the "fuzzy boundaries" of some of our categories of experience—as those of color—testify. Therefore, we could argue that Goodenough's notion of "learned response" to stimuli involves by necessity a measure of selectivity in the quest for salience, particularly in evidence where contrast may be hard to fathom.

This is precisely the kind of insight we can also glean from analyses of the experience of sound and its signification. I will argue that the perceiving of *experience* in terms of categories is an activity that depends on silence for its success. Phonemes are an apt example of this activity, for their "objectification" can be understood as a primary experience of perception, and not only as a second-level elaboration through language.[2]

How Sounds Become Phonemes

References to the term *phoneme* go back to the end of the nineteenth century when linguists from a variety of perspectives and localities, often unaware of one another's work, understood that there are sounds and then there is the perception of sounds. Which perception ends up subdividing, for all practical purposes, the emission of sounds into minimal units—or bundles of items—of significance; themselves variously recognized by speakers and nonspeakers of a language.[3]

Several aspects of the analysis of phonemes are relevant here, primary among them the understanding that phonemic identity does not depend on rigidity of boundaries, but rather on degrees of salience assigned to a variety of relevant elements. Though intended as a tool to help us simplify and clarify the complexity of the sound production/sound perception tie, phonemes have been a remarkably slippery concept; seen by some as bundles of distinctive features (Jakobson in Pike 1967: 348), as bent on overlapping one another (Bloch in Pike 1967: 348), or as consisting of a multiplicity of cues (Ferguson discussing Halle in Pike 1967: 348); a degree of phonemic ambiguity which has invited an analogy with physics, as in Pike's envisioning such minimal units as "particles," "waves," or "fields" (1976: 93). Pike verbalized best the quandary of the phonemic enterprise:

> ... I have found it necessary, in an empirical view, to treat segments of sound—phones—as having determinate centers, but indeterminate borders... Other scholars of the time were more inclined to try to assume that a segment was determinate, and define phones in reference to its borders. *I avoided this deliberately since the borders were in fact empirically often not detectable by ear or instrument* (1976: 98, emphasis added).

Sound is not as simple and as self-evident as it appears. Discreteness in phonemes may only fully exist if we focus on the "center" of each phone, the point at which the sound is most distinctively itself, most contrastive, while the margins are lost in indeterminacy.[4]

Recognizing the distinction between phones and phonemes accomplishes a couple of tasks. First of all, the arbitrariness of sound perception is underlined. For units of agreed upon contrast are the *speakers' interpretation* of what constitutes contrast, which, while indeed it does reflect contrast, does not encompass all contrast that is present—though unremarked as carrier of significance. Most tellingly, it points to the *concrete physicality of silence*; which physicality is present in each variation in "value"[5] of the same phoneme—as reflected in the range of acoustic cues that it encompasses.

What is of interest, for our purposes, can be described as the perceptual homogenizing of all allophones into one phoneme by speakers of a language and, conversely, the ability of non-speakers to register them as discrete—if such distinction happens to exist in the observer's own linguistic context.[6] In either case, the ghost of *silent sounds* persists.

This widens the scope of Goodenough's point that phonemes are "conceptually discrete, even if their concrete articulation is occasionally fuzzily ambiguous"(1999:25); for I will argue that such discreteness out of fuzzy ambiguity can take place only if we take into account the notion of silence, a notion meant to reflect the experience of absence-in-presence in the perception of sound.

The issue of *selective hearing* has certainly been central for those concerned with problems of transcription and of translation—as Pike was. I will argue that it is also central to issues of agency and—ultimately—of power. For if we accept that, even at the level of sound, significance involves something other than mechanical registering; that it involves a selection of sorts, whether from the insider's perspective—as with the experience of allophones—or from the outsider's perspective—as with "hard to hear" /r/ in Japanese or hard to hear /th/ in English; further, if we accept that such selectivity functions by effectively erasing a part of reality—in sounds that exist but are not "heard" if not part of one's linguistic context—then we can argue that *meaning* is dependent on the ability to mute an aspect of reality in order to foreground another. In this case, selectivity resides in the perception of acoustic cues in phonemes; which includes not picking up some cues, and/or picking them up but not attaching significance to them.

This is relevant because it throws light on the role of both speaker and hearer as agents in the meaning construction process, and on the contexts that set the parameters for the activation of their agency.

Context and Agency

The existence of language-specific receptivity of acoustic cues suggests that our perceptive capabilities are wider than their linguistic actualizations. Belonging to a speech community entails that we streamline our wide capabilities, polymorphic with respect to sound, polysemic with respect to meaning, into accepted patterns of reception as well as production of

sound, significance, and meaning. As Schumann has vividly put it, while the human brain is programmed to evaluate stimuli in terms of their intrinsic familiarity / pleasantness—and their converse—such ability is "captured" by "society" and bent to its needs/desires, which in turn will impact the individual's appraisal of stimuli (1999: 21).[7] Or, in Pike's words, "language goes deep" (1977: 119). It provides us with patterns for hearing as well as for speaking. It sets in motion our ability to tune into the world around us or overlook it. And the channels for this reside, in the first instance, in our ability to selectively recognize, absorb, and tune out the constant noise in which we are immersed.

I will argue that the conceptual discreteness of phonemes, which takes place notwithstanding the fluidity of stimuli that underlies them, results in their seeming perceptual discreteness. For the phonemic categories themselves guide our experience into the necessary parameters; and they do so by glossing over some stimulus inputs which become irrelevant, though they do not disappear.

It is not only that "shifts in what one categorizes the same sensory or information inputs changes what one perceives"—as Goodenough has argued (1999: 26). Rather, the very language-specific activity of selection of relevant elements and muting of other elements which are not deemed central *channels* our experience: it squeezes it into the appropriate parameters; which propriety differs with different linguistic contexts.

In the final analysis, the condition of discreteness involves an arbitrary boundary marker that distinguishes each unit from any other such unit of signification, even in the face of actual fluidity. We need such a concept of boundary with its implication of internal homogeneity, or at least congruence, if we are to rely on the consistency of signification of any unit. Beyond each boundary of internal consistency is otherness. That such boundary be theoretical, at best, does not minimize its functionality; rather it underlines its silent dimension.

Silence, then, refers to our understanding that meaning is dependent for its formation on the seeming integrity of the sounds that carry it: it is the concept we need to have in order to trust that /p/ and /b/ stand in relationship of contrast to one another rather than as two ranges in a continuum of bilabial aspiration. As such, silence is the necessary ingredient for the active creation of contrast in sound, a contrast which is much less evident in the experience than in the ideology of sound perception—as the analysis of "phonemes" illustrates.

Hence silence is the cradle for the birth of meaning. For only when the sounds we have learned to group under /p/ and /b/ can be heard as non-

/b/ and non-/p/ respectively—however porous their borders might be—can we use each for the construction of *pit* and *bit* as meaningful concepts. But /p/ and /b/ an be heard as significantly different only when we willfully disregard our ability to hear each of the two phonemes as a bundle of sounds and hear it instead as an *umbrella sound* for a number of possible variations.

We have then two activities taking place at the same time. One activity gathers a number of shifts of sound under an umbrella sound-concept we learn to identify as *the* sound, or the significant sound, or the locus of contrast in sounds, or the center of a sound. And a second activity, taking place contemporarily, erases from our consciousness the relevance—if not the existence—of the sound variation that stands as our "umbrella" of recognized significance, effectively silencing the variation. Therefore, at the heart of our meaning construction process is an act of suppression: hence the need to look at agency in such a process.

A final and parallel process is one of mystification; where the silencing of contrast inherent in voicing is mistaken for absence, for non existence of variation, which allows for the denial of competing experience as well as invites the essentializing of the self, however marked.

Agency and Selective Hearing

Issues of agency inform the analysis of "speech acts" as described by Austin. In a series of lectures delivered at Harvard in 1955, Austin explained his notion that speech is ultimately action. First, and most subtly, he pointed out what he called the "descriptive fallacy" (1962: 3) of analyses that overlook the importance of context in the exchange of seemingly straightforward sentences; for the intentions of the speaker can turn a seemingly descriptive sentence into a command, into a request for complicity or, minimally, for compliance. Most glaringly, Austin underlined the existence of sentences that *are* themselves an action, rather than the description of one; sentences such as "I do" in a marriage ceremony or "I bet" in play. However, here too, in order for these utterances to be "performative" of action, they must be uttered in the right context: seriously, in the proper place, and so on (1962: lecture I).

What is important, for our purposes, is twofold. First, words are deemed to be inherently tied up with action, as opposed to being limited to a description of action, both because they provoke action and because they constitute action. Most significantly, such action depends on the intentions of the speaker. If the intentions are *off* the action is void. That Austin calls these the "infelicities" or "unhappinesses" of speech acts tells us something about his assessment of their role. Intentions are at the center of speech acts, and their break-down subverts the very speech act, hence erases the boundaries of meaning. Infelicities affect all sorts of utterances, in Austin's view. For even straightforward "statement utterances" can be plagued by lies or "insincerities" (1962: lecture II).

Here too, there is a silent dimension to meaning. Such silent dimension is evident in all those instances when intentionality alters the context for the successful functioning of meaning in utterances to such an extent as to subvert it. And it does so by fudging or erasing the basic guidelines for the successful delivery of meaningful utterances, *while leaving their expression intact.*

When we highlight the boundaries within which utterances must function in order to be meaningful—as Austin does—we are envisioning a space of non-meaning beyond such boundary; but not—as Austin points out—of nonexistence of speech. The utterances are expressed; they are heard. What is missing is the successful transferal of meaning: a semantic silence of sorts.

This is an exact parallel of the phonemic analysis engaged earlier: the role of silence becomes apparent if we consider how meaning is constructed in primary instances of communication when sounds are heard as categories and intentions mark the action of speech.

The point here is that not only is language a tool for "doing"[8] as well as an action itself in its information capacity. Rather, language is the product of an activity. The major aspect of which activity is a process of obfuscation, be it of phonic variation or of divergent intentions, by means of which we deny reality in order to construct it. Hence we act as though perceivable, and, indeed, perceived phonic variation did not exist and intentions were always transparent.

In our guise as hearers we are not the passive member of a speech dyad in which the agent is the speaker. Rather, we are active participants in the construction of meaning both because we "implicitly agree on what the speaker counts as having done"—as Sbisá has put it (1999: 10), as well as—I have argued—by agreeing to overlook some stimuli; those which our linguistic context does not direct us to perceive as significant. In her critique of Austin, Sbisá notes that the speaker's intents are achieved only if they are received as such. My point is that the receiving itself only works if there is an active silencing of perception. To put it in Austin's terminology, the act of hearing produces a performative whose "felicity" rests on successful muting.

If agency be "the human capacity to act," as some have noted (Ahearn 1999: 12), agency is at the heart of silence as participants in speech acts fail to hear just those stimuli which they must overlook—given their linguistic contexts. Therefore, hearers are integral agents to the meaning construction process, through selective hearing, which inheres selective suppression of sound variation; in other words: silence. Not only are all utterances "performatives" in their role as carriers of information, as Austin has argued, but all perceptions can be seen as performatives in their role as suppressors of variation in the search for salience.

As an activity, such obfuscation and muting of extant stimuli in order to foreground those permitted by the context is both universal and contingent, as the great variety of linguistic contexts testifies.

Silence and Potentiality

The existence of arbitrariness in speech—from its most basic building blocks of sound to its most complex level of semantics—is only possible if there is selectivity and suppression in perception, which points to a domain repository of the unselected, unfocused, unprivileged: a domain of silent sounds, silent meanings, silent structures.

Because silence is experienced as absence, it is interpreted as nonexistence and tied to negativity. Rather, I will argue, the tacit dimension is illustrative and, perhaps, even evidence of potentiality. When we identify a sound as significant and relegate another into oblivion; when we recognize the meaning of only some utterances and not others we are building our capacity to experience the world and react to it over and above sound. And to the extent that we are the product of our perceptions, propelled by our experiences—sensory or otherwise—this linguistic dance of choice of relevance ends up being our self; a self that can be lost in a foreign context—as those who have experienced exile have reminded us.[9] This may help explain the heavy psychic toll exacted by nonfamiliar linguistic contexts described by Pike with such passion:

> Once more I felt deep cultural shock, a deep bitter nausea welling up as if to spew out in rage revolt at all foreign customs, sounds, words which seemed to be invading to desecrate my very soul. Language goes deep. (1977: 119)

Because the building of reliable significance involves a selection, which selection comports a tacit reeling into oblivion of all that is potentially perceivable, but is not perceived because irrelevant to the linguistic context or veiled by a communicative intent, we are always attempting to eliminate the echoes of other possibilities. For other possibilities comport other syntheses of self, as well as of sound: hence the rage described by Pike; a rage at having to fish out of silence the bait of discarded possibilities—of sound, of significance, of meaning. In translation, we become anglers of silence. And we do that because identity, any identity, would not exist but for the silencing of potential otherness—of sound, of meaning, of speech, which allows it to be voiced and recognized.

Hence the power of silence resides, in the last instance, in the role that silence plays in the construction of the self by means of the suppression of competing significance.

Because, as we have seen, such suppression depends on our willingness to believe in absence-in-presence, a final space which silence unleashes is one of mystification: a central ingredient for the essentializing of self and of others.

Silence's power resides in the paradoxical situation where the matrix of presence is experienced as absence. Much like Zero for the language of numbers, silence functions as bestower of meaning in the interplay between negativity and potentiality.[10]

Wider Implications: Silence and Race

I will argue that the activity of meaning construction out of competing potential significance by means of suppression of experience constitutes a system of habitual practices that undergirds all identity formation: what Bourdieu has labeled "habitus" whose role or "fundamental effect" is precisely "the production of a commonsense world." And such commonsense world, we are told, derives its "objectivity" from the redundancy and predictability of common or parallel experiences (Bourdieu 1977: 80).

The contention here is that the practices centered on *silence* which forge our experience into categories that foreground consistency where there is flux, salience where there is continuity, and hence point to *selective/arbitrary*, as opposed to inherent/inevitable, discreteness are the lynchpin in our experience of other categories of identity over and above sound. For in any identity, the need for consistency and salience requires isolating contrast where there is continuity, homogeneity where there is variation. Yet the fact that these are observable practices clearly indicates that even knowledge of the neutral kind can be shown to be demonstrably constructed: from the sound up.

Some categories of identity are experienced as foundational precisely because the agency and self-interest that underlies *all* identity formation has been successfully veiled and such identity has claimed to be a reflection rather than a construction of reality.

Power and Racial Identity

This understanding is at the heart of the critique of race as a category of identity and of attempts to deconstruct it. It has been argued that the markers of racial discreteness are product of a search for salience which has selected some elements of biology, genetic inheritance and behavior as diagnostic of group membership and ignored others that would undermine such discreteness (Smedley 1998). Such process of construction of salience can be pinpointed in time and has involved very different contexts (Shanklin 1994, Takaki 1993). And it persists as "the problem of the 20th century" (Harrison 1998: 609). This occurs notwithstanding what we know about the clinal condition of gene flow and genetic inheritance (Templeton 1998, Cartmill 1998) such as the *myth* of phenotypic similarity as indicative of genotypic similarity (Templeton 1998), or the role of environment in genetic inheritance (Cartmill 1998), evident even in those variations traditionally thought to be racially marked—as sickle cell, for example (Livingstone in Harrison 1998: 615); as well as is contrary to what we know about the actual fluidity of racial categories (Valdez and Valdez 1998).

Hence, race as category of identity has been understood as a veritable construction of self and of otherness whose causes have been seen to reside in a variety of loci of material and ideological self-interest ranging from wide hegemonic projects at the service of a capitalist mode of production (Wolf 1982), or of a plantation economy (Takaki 1993), to a partisan political agenda from "the right" (Omi & Winant 1986). These race-based projects have been achieved by means of the "biologizing" power of the state, manifested in the politics of both race and sexuality (Stoler 1995). These economic and political agenda continue to rely on a segmented consciousness of the labor force (Wolf 1982, 1994) as well as on the privilege available to those involved in such biologizing enterprise that cloaks issues of power in biological garb; a privilege that covers both those who engage in it (Cartmill 1998), and how it is funded (Harrison 1998). All of

which is compounded by the survival needs of physical anthropology departments (Cartmill 1998) as well as by the timidity of cultural anthropologists who are not willing to recognize that teaching is a form of action, minimally in the communication of transforming ideas, such as those regarding the constructedness of race (Shanklin, 1998).

This suggests that race has been a unit of significance in a language developed to concretize otherness in order to create and maintain privilege.

Silence and the Power of Race

Two aspects of the analysis of race outlined above are particularly pertinent here. The first is that, notwithstanding its early interrogation and its current deconstruction, the concept of *race* as a category of identity survives and prospers both in and out of academia. The second and related issue is that there is a disjunction between the scholarly and the folk views of race, and paradigm shifts in the former do not seem to penetrate the wider collective consciousness.

I will submit that the road to understanding the phoenix-like nature of race, that seems unfazed by our deconstructionist zeal, is to view it through the prism of the *silence habitus* of meaning-construction; by means of which any and all identity is the product of a silencing process based on selective suppression—as well as choice—of relevance at the service of salience dictated by the needs of the contexts; hence, in which self-interest looms large.

From this perspective we can see that *race* rests on a system of practices deeply embedded in silence in terms of both its experience and its analysis. For, in order to recognize racial distinctions, we must suppress what we experience of human variability and focus on the salience of traits we have learned to identify as markers of discreteness. We also must mute what we know of biology and genetic inheritance, about history and the flexibility of behavior, as we have seen.

The effects of such practices of meaning construction through suppression have also been marked by silence, as the essentialized others are effectively silenced by being severed from access to resources (Wolf 1982), and literally silenced as their cognition is put in doubt (Shanklin 1994) and their speech undervalued (Hill 1998). Their very experience of racism can be effectively muzzled by the "cultural censorship" that sustains hegemonic systems (Sheriff 2000).

From this critical perspective, race is a (phon-)eme-like concept in the etic domain of human (bio-behavioral) variability. As such it functions as a measure of significance in the establishment of group inclusion and exclusion. While rising out of the material and ideological needs of domination, racial identity ends up determining degrees of access to resources of all kinds. Therefore, though based on the interpretation of biological (dis)connectedness, *race* is a building block in the language of power, not in the language of biology.[11]

It has already been noted that "construals of language" can give rise to the "naturalization" of social difference (Errington 1999: 115). The contention here is that such process starts in the very first instance of linguistic experience, that of sound and its interpretation/internalization as phoneme, with its attendant silence and silencing potential; with the practices that allow us to hear and not hear, thereby registering only that which is in our communicative interest. Which become part and parcel of "schemes of perception, conception, and action....[that constitute] the precondition for all objectification and apperception"—-as Bourdieu has verbalized it (1977: 86).

We are, then, confronted with the production of meaning at the expense of experience and with the creation of experience from the meanings we have thus produced.

This is not neutral even as a process of primary meaning formation, as we have seen: issues of self-interest always underlie it. From the vantage point of phonemes and speech acts, the *self* is the specific linguistic context whose *interest* lies in communicability of meaning; from the vantage point of other foundational categories of identity the contexts are given by the shifting parameters of self-interest of the agents involved in the jostling of power, affected differently in different contexts by the interplay between ideological and material concerns.

This may help to explain the vitality of race as a category of identity. For, on the one hand, the stress on homogeneity and discreteness in identity does not erase the reality of variation, present as it is in each exception, in each marginal case or in the classifications of others or of other times: hence the deconstructionist push. On the other hand, recognizing the constructedness of essence does not erase from our minds the internalization of the category. Nor does it eliminate the practice of identification of self and others, though the parameters of self-interest may shift.

Once in existence, categories of identity appear inherent over and above their function as displacement mechanism in the distancing of outgroups.[12] Rather, they acquire a life of their own because the practices of silence in which they are embedded shape our parameters of perceptions, constantly reinforcing the categorical boundaries. Hence we continue to experience the salience of those traits that are presupposed by our categories—just as we continue to fully hear only the sounds that are significant in our linguistic context. Understanding the arbitrariness of our categories of identity does not preclude our ability to pick up the distinctions we have learned to isolate as significant—be they sounds or phenotypes.

Propelled by the silence habitus and political agenda, all manner of categories of identity have served our interest; producing both imagined communities of imputed similarity (Anderson 1983), and the solace of "cultural intimacy" in identification (Herzfeld 1997), even as they have given rise to racially marked hierarchies of access which in the American context have equated privilege with whiteness (Frankenberg 1993) and whiteness with full citizenship (Takaki 1993). In fact, the deep-seated unfairness of such inequities may be impossible to address but with recourse to the language of race and its arbitrary demarcations at the service of power (Baker 1998).

In the complexity of race and its deconstruction we find the outlines of an analytical trap where engagement and observation appear at loggerheads. From an analytical perspective we must avoid being caught between essentialist positions that sacrifice our knowledge and our very experience of human variation in order to stress racial discreteness, thereby reinforcing the very hierarchy of inequality which has produced it and a deconstruction that flirts with denying the essentializing effects of history in the name of exposing its ideological dimension, thereby impeding its redress and sowing distrust on the authenticity of in-group identification.

Focusing on silence allows us to avoid both pitfalls by turning our attention to the process of essence formation that takes place in our practices of making meaning and to the selectivity the making of meaning inheres.

Notes

1. The notion of foundational identity was developed by Nina Glick Schiller in the issue titled "Foundational Concepts: Gender. Race, and Locality" of her journal, *Identities.*
2. While Goodenough's example of color categories is less convincing, for it is not clear whether we are being presented with "fuzzy boundary" of perception or "fuzzy boundary" in the "objectivizing" of such perception through language, the hypothesis

that perception be not a given, but an activity, stands, and it can be supported more adequately with an examination of the perception of sound and its internalization into phonemes. Goodenough does talk of phonemes, but his interest is in showing how phonemes are constituted by other "categories"—sound categories—in an effort to show the grid-like interfacing of categories; each of which can be seen as a set; hence, phonemes are constituted by sound categories, themselves distinguished and rendered discrete by their "focal points of references," whether or not their articulation is clear or fuzzy. Whereas I argue that "phonemes" were intended as a tool to describe our selective perception of sound, not only our definition of the same.

3. European and American linguists tended to view them as systems of opposition and systems of units, respectively.
4. Experiments with four-month-old infants conducted in 1971 by Einar R. Siqueland, Peter W. Jusczyk, James Vigorito, and Peter Eimas placed the recognition of discreteness in phonemes at the thirty milliseconds mark of voice-onset time indicating that: "no single value of voice-onset time defines each phoneme ... hearers typically perceive a range of values reflecting different speakers, different instances of speech and differences in the surrounding phonemic environment, as examples of the same phoneme." (Eimas 1985: 118)
5. As used by Eimas (ibid).
6. Examples of this would be /r/ and /l/ for Japanese and English speakers, respectively, and /t/ and /th/ for English and Nepali speakers, respectively.
7. Such triangulation has come to us early with Saussure's view of the role of the *masse parlante* in determining the tie between signifier and signified within a sign, a tie which is un-motivated, structurally crucial, and determined by factors outside the sign—-such as contrast with other signs as well as speakers—in an unspecified manner (1968).
8. I am using Sbisá's verbalization of Austin's performatives.
9. See Eva Hoffman (1989) for an evocative discussion of the loss of self accompanying involuntary migration and immersion into an alien language.
10. See Georges Ifrah's (1994) discussion of "zero" as the point of departure of mathematics: the insight which made it possible to step from nothingness to the operations on numerical units.
11. Were we to use genetic inheritance as the basis for discreteness in social groups, we would need to posit the existence of 1,000,000 such discrete groups (Cavalli-Sforza 2000: 30).
12. This is not a new understanding; see a good discussion of this issue in Allport (1954).

References Cited

Ahearn, Laura M. 1999. "Agency." *Journal of Linguistic Anthropology* 9(1-2): 12-15.

Allport, Gordon. 1954. *The Nature of Prejudice.* Cambridge,Mass.: Addison-Wesley Publishing.

Anderson, Benedict. 1983. *Imagined Communities: Reflections on the Origins and Spread of Nationalism.* New York: Verso.

Austin, John L. 1962. *How to Do Things with Words.* Oxford: Oxford University Press.

Baker, Lee D. 1998. *From Savage to Negro: Anthropology and the Construction of Race, 1896-1954.* Berkeley: University of California Press.

Bourdieu, Pierre. 1977. *Outline of a Theory of Practice.* Cambridge: Cambridge University Press.

Cartmill, Matt. 1998. "The Status of the Race Concept in Physical Anthropology." *American Anthropologist* 100(3): 651-660.

Cavalli-Sforza, Luigi Luca. 2000. *Genes, People, and Languages.* New York: North Point Press.

Eimas, Peter. 1985. "The Perception of Speech in Early Infancy." In *The Emergence of Language Development and Evolution.* William S-Y. Wang, ed., 117-127. New York: H. Freeman and Company.

Errington, Joseph.1999. "Ideology." *Journal of Linguistic Anthropology* 9(1-2): 115-117

Ervin-Tripp, Susan.1999. "Acquisition." *Journal of Linguistic Anthropology* 9(1-2): 6-8.

Frankenberg, Ruth. 1993. *White Women, Race Matter: The Social Construction of Whitness.* Minneapolis: University of Minnesota Press.

Gibson, Kathleen R. 1999. "Evolution." *Journal of Linguistic Anthropology* 9(1-2): 69-71.

Goodenough, Ward H. 1999. "Category." *Journal of Linguistic Anthropology* 9(1-2): 24-27.

Harrison, Faye V. 1998. "Introduction: Expanding the Discourse on Race." *American Anthropologist* 100(3): 609-631.

Herzfeld, Michael. 1997. *Cultural Intimacy: Social Poetics in the Nation-State.* New York: Rutledge.

Hill, Jane. 1998. "Language, Race and White Public Space." *American Anthropologist* 100(3): 680-689.

Hoffman, Eva. 1989. *Lost in Translation: A Life in a New Language.* New York: Penguin Books.

Ifrah, Georges. 1994. *Histoire Universelle des Chiffres*. Paris: France Loisirs (Editions Robert Laffont).
Kay, Paul. 1999. "Color." *Journal of Linguistic Anthropology* 9(1-2): 32-35.
Omi, Michael and Howard Winant. 1986. *Racial Formation in the United States: From the 1960s to the 1980s*. New York: Routledge.
Pike, Kenneth. 1967. *Language in Relation to a Unified Theory of the Structure of Human Behavior*. The Hague: Mouton.
_____ 1976. "Theoretical Discussion." In *Tagmemics, Volume 2*. Ruth Brend and Kenneth Pike, eds. The Hague: Mouton.
_____ 1977. *Songs of Fun and Faith by Fish and Chip*. Lake Bluff, Ill.: Jupiter Press.
Saussure, Ferdinand de. [1916]1968. *Cours de Linguistique Generale*. Gottingen: Hubert & Co.
Sbisá, Marina. 1999. "Act." *Journal of Linguistic Anthropology* 9(1-2): 9-11.
Schiller, Nina Glick. 1998. "The More Things Change… ?" *Identities: Global Studies in Culture and Power* 5 (3): 297-299.
Schumann, John H. 1999. "Brain." *Journal of Linguistic Anthropology* 9(1-2): 20-23.
Shanklin, Eugenia. 1994. *Anthropology and Race*. Belmont, Ca: Wadsworth.
_____ 1998. "The Profession of the Color Blind: Sociocultural Anthropology and Racism in the 21st Century." *American Anthropologist* 100: 669-679.
Sheriff, Robin E. 2000. "Exposing Silence as Cultural Censorship: A Brazilian Case." *American Anthropologist* 102(1): 114-132.
Smedley Audrey. 1998. "Race and the Construction of Human Identity." *American Anthropologist* 100(3): 690-702.
Stoler, Ann Laura. 1995. *Race and the Education of Desire*. Durham, NC: Durham University Press.
Takaki, Ronald. 1993. *A Different Mirror: A History of Multicultural America*. Boston: Little Brown.
Templeton, Alan R. 1998. "Human Races: A Genetic and Evolutionary Perspective." *American Anthropologist* 100(3): 632-650.
Valdez, Norberto and Janice Valdez. 1998. "The Pot that Called the Kettle White: Changing Racial Identities and U.S. Social Construction of Race." *Identities* 5 (3): 375-413.
Wolf, Eric R. 1982. *Europe and the People without History*. Berkeley: University of California Press.

_____ 1994. "Perilous Ideas: Race, Culture, People." *Current Anthropology* 35(1):1-12.

_____ (with Sydel Silverman). 2001. "Facing Power: Old Insights, New Questions." In *Pathways of Power: Building an Anthropology of the Modern World.* Berkeley: University of California Press.

Chapter 3

Language Policies and the Erasure of Multilingualism in South Africa[1]

Susan E. Cook

Introduction

South Africa's celebrated transition from apartheid to liberal democracy since 1994 has, in part, been organized around the ideas of reconciling racial groups that were previously pitted against one another, and achieving a new and official sense of equity among the society's ethnic groupings, some privileged and others disadvantaged by the apartheid system. Curiously, though, the effort to reverse the racial and ethnic segregation of apartheid has, in some ways, had the effect of reinscribing the very boundaries and categories it seeks to annul. A good example of this is the language policies being implemented by the present government of South Africa. Despite the worthy aims of protecting and supporting the use of previously disadvantaged languages and using language to promote both unity and diversity in the new South Africa, close scrutiny reveals that the language policies of the new government, and the concepts that buttress them, serve instead to symbolically erase fundamental social realities in contemporary South African society.

In particular, this chapter examines the relationship of national language policies to ground level language practices. The language repertoires and actual speech behaviors of people living in a township in North West Province are contrasted with the language policies in their schools, and on their TVs and radios. To the extent that the official language policies do not reflect the lived realities of people in this region, I will ask what assumptions about language, ethnicity, and nationhood underpin these policies and enable people to "make sense" of the gap between language policy and language practice. I employ the semiotic concept of "erasure" to theorize the ideological process that takes place when certain dominant ideas, through their implicit assumptions and discursive force, render invisible particular social phenomena, including speech behavior.

One of the most important (and one of the least interrogated) ideas that have formed the ideological basis for a great number of policies (language and otherwise) in South Africa over the years is that of unitary and bounded languages/cultures/territories. This idea, rooted strongly in the German Intellectual Romantic movement of the eighteenth century, came to South Africa with the European missionaries who began arriving in South Africa in large numbers in the early nineteenth century (Fabian 1986, Comaroff and Comaroff 1991). This school of thought is centered on the idea that a nation or race of people is indivisible from its language and territory (Herder 1966), and that an individual carries the whole of his or her culture, language, and national essence within him or her (von Humboldt 1988). Thus the Xhosa and the Zulu, while speaking closely related languages, were considered separate peoples, as well as the Sotho and Tswana, whose regional dialects, it can be argued, form a single continuum rather than two distinct languages (Janson & Tsonope 1991, Willan 1996). Although Herder's influential writings did not envision ethnolinguistic boundaries as the grounds for political nationalism, his ideas have been deployed, consciously or not, in the service of this cause (Tambiah 1996). His idea that a group's memory, culture, and history are all of a piece led the way to anti-Enlightenment projects such as the Afrikaner *volkstad* premised on the need to preserve the unity and purity of "the nation" by all means possible (Templin 1984, Moodie 1975).

The European missionaries who penetrated the South African interior in the early nineteenth century came not only to convert local people to Christianity, but also to "discover" and study the human landscape. They identified ethnic groups, codified languages, and mapped the territory according to discrete "tribes" or "nations" whose boundaries did not overlap, and whose linguistic, ethnic, and territorial distinctness was implicit (Harries 1988). These "scientific discoveries" by Europeans in the pre colonial period have had long-lasting effect, in that they established the conceptual grounds not only for the institution of separate black "homelands" under apartheid, but also for the official language policies of the new democratic South Africa.

The South African Constitution of 1996 enshrines eleven official languages, including the two former official languages, English and Afrikaans, and nine "historically marginalized" languages.[2] The country's official language statement is found in Section One of Founding Provision Six in the Constitution, and as such, is the preeminent statement of the government's approach to language. That is, all specific language policies that are developed and implemented to redress past inequalities in South Africa must flow from, and be in accordance with, the policy of eleven official languages, also referred to as "the principle of multilingualism" (Government of South Africa 2003).

Founding Provision Six also articulates additional principles that govern the development of language policy in South Africa. These include making the state responsible for strengthening the historically disadvantaged languages (including Setswana); mandating that the government must conduct its own business using all of the official languages; and creating a Pan South African Language Board that should concern itself not only with the eleven official languages, but also with the various other languages spoken by South Africans, such as South African sign language.

A recent piece of legislation entitled the "South African Languages Bill" seeks to operationalize Founding Provision Six with three major policy initiatives. The first is a set of regulations for publishing government documents. This policy requires government bodies to publish any public document in four of the eleven official languages, one from each of four categories, and to rotate among the languages in each group.

The second policy requirement is the creation of a "language unit" for each department of the national government and for each province, both to implement language policies that are in line with the government's overall objectives, as well as to field responses, complaints, and so forth, from the public regarding language issues. The third policy requirement names the Minister of the Department of Arts, Culture, Science, and Technology as the person responsible for developing indigenous South African languages.

While these initiatives seem innovative, fair, and intended to empower those who were previously deprived of rights by the repressive apartheid regime, the assumptions on which they're based come straight out of Herderian linguistics. Equating social equality with linguistic equality (which is, in effect, what Founding Provision Six does), and asserting that the best way to promote South African culture is to protect and preserve eleven distinct groupings, is equivalent to serving old wine in new bottles.

On a practical level, one of the bill's greatest limitations is that it does not establish jurisdiction over language policies in education or in commercial broadcasting. It is in the schools, after all, that questions of a language's status, content, and domains of use have a direct impact on society. And it is to television and radio that the vast majority of South Africans turn to for information, entertainment, and images of themselves and the world (Spitulnik 2001). It is for this reason that this chapter focuses on the approach of educators and broadcasters to language questions. As will become clear, the Ministry of Education and the provincial education authorities operate under the same assumptions and principles as those who drafted the Constitution, while TV and radio broadcasters represent an alternate vision of language use in South Africa today.

Language Practices in Tlhabane Township

Before looking at specific language policies in education and broadcasting, it is important to have an overview of people's actual language behavior. The contrasts between how people communicate using language and the assumptions about language embedded in the official language policies will provide the basis for discussion for the remainder of the chapter.

North West Province is one of nine provinces in South Africa and comprises what was, under the apartheid administrative divisions, the Western Transvaal and most of the quasi-independent Bophuthatswana "bantustan," purported home to most of South Africa's ethnic Tswanas. Although the majority of people in North West Province do, in fact, identify as ethnic Tswanas, there are large numbers of Pedis, Sothos, and Afrikaners as well. Smaller concentrations of Anglophone whites, Coloureds, South Asians, Zulus, Xhosas, Shangaans, and members of other ethnic groups also live in the region (Black Sash 1990). The focus of this chapter is the majority Tswana group, the historical inhabitants of this region.

Adjacent to Gauteng Province, where Johannesburg and Pretoria are located, the North West Province is mostly made up of towns, townships, villages, and large tracts of agricultural land. Near the town of Rustenburg lies Tlhabane, a black township built as a labor reserve in the early 1900s. Tlhabane is a typical example of the ethnically and racially segregated reserves that the apartheid regime built to serve the labor needs of nearby white-owned farms, industry, and residential areas. Although the inhabitants of Tlhabane are mostly ethnic Tswanas, there are also many Xhosas, Zulus, Shangaans, Sothos, Pedis, and people from neighboring countries who migrate to this region to find work in the nearby platinum and chrome mines. Socio-economically diverse, as well as ethnically heterogeneous, Tlhabane has affluent neighborhoods where the homes have two-car garages and swimming pools, as well as desperately poor neighborhoods where the residents live in crowded and squalid conditions.

Although it is located in the heart of historically Setswana-speaking territory, Tlhabane has always been a place where a range of languages have been used. In the 1950s, Breutz reported, "the vernacular in the location is the Native language, mainly Setswana, although most of the Natives know some Afrikaans or English" (Breutz 1953: 48-49). Most of the individuals interviewed in the course of my research command an even broader range of languages.[3] The following brief profiles describe the language repertoires and general circumstances of some typical residents of Tlhabane. Ezra,[4] sixty-five, has lived most of his life in the rural areas, but came to Tlhabane in the 1980s to find work as a plumber. He speaks Setswana and Afrikaans fluently, as well as a little English. He also speaks Tsotsitaal (a non-standard variety of Afrikaans that indexes urbanity and masculinity amongst its speakers), and some Xhosa and Zulu. His home—a twelve by fifteen foot corrugated iron shack with no windows, electricity, or plumbing—is located in the oldest and poorest part of the township, appropriately named "Ou Kassie" ("old location" in Afrikaans). Ezra and his family share one outhouse and one standpipe for water with thirty to forty other people.

In the central part of the township, Frances, thirty-three, lives alone in a roomy shack that stands behind a house that doubles as a *shebeen* (an unlicensed bar usually located in someone's home). Frances moved to Tlhabane in 1990 to work at the Tlhabane Sun, a hotel and gambling casino on the edge of the township. Frances finished high school and studied towards a diploma in business. She is a native speaker of Setswana, but also speaks fluent Afrikaans, English, Zulu, and Xhosa, more often in combination than one at a time.

Fox Lake is one of the newer, more upscale, sections of Tlhabane. It has no shacks, but rather four and six room brick houses with lawns and driveways. It has a suburban feel, and is the neighborhood of choice for businesspeople, teachers, and civil servants. Mr. Tau is a primary school principal, and lives in Fox Lake with his wife and son. He speaks Setswana and English.

Mr. and Mrs. Mmutle live in Bester, the most affluent section of the township, with spacious homes and well-manicured lawns. Although predominantly Tswana-speaking like the rest of Tlhabane's residents, many children from Bester (including the Mmutles') attend private "multiracial" (i.e., English medium) schools in nearby Rustenburg. The Mmutles, both educators, use English for most of their daily interactions, but believe strongly in the symbolic importance of their mother tongue, Setswana.

What all of these people share is native fluency in Setswana, while the other languages in their individual repertoires are the result of their personal histories and circumstances. In general, few blacks in North West speak fewer than three languages, and most have a passive understanding of two or three more. This is true of men and women, young and old, rich and poor, and to a lesser extent, both urban and rural dwellers.

This degree of multilingualism is not uncommon among black South Africans, or, indeed, among Africans on many parts of the continent. The legacy of colonialism, the phenomenon of language contact, the institution of labor migration, and the politics of racial segregation have all contributed to people's extensive linguistic repertoires. Many people find themselves using one language variety at home, another one (or two) in school, a lingua franca designed for communication among people of different ethnic and national origins in the mines (Fanakalo—see Adendorff 1995), and yet another speech form in their social interactions with their peers. It is therefore not uncommon for people in Tlhabane to use three or four different languages in the course of a single day.

In addition to the prevalence of multilingualism in this region, however, is the fact of widespread *multidialectalism*, or the command of more than one dialect of a language. In a context such as Tlhabane, it is tempting to take people's shared identity as Setswana speakers for granted and focus instead on the variation in their knowledge of different "languages," e.g., English, Afrikaans, Zulu, and so on. In fact, however, very few people even use standard Setswana at all. Instead, they use a complex array of non standard forms of Setswana that not only reflect the current political, economic, and cultural realities in urban South Africa, but also are deployed in strategic ways to shape them.

The variety of Setswana that people speak differs from the standard dialect mostly in its lexicon. "Street Setswana" incorporates lexical items from a wide range of other languages, including English, Afrikaans, Zulu, and Tsotsitaal (Cook 1999). Better described as a range of styles than as a single language or dialect (i.e., a well defined and bounded code with a unique grammar, morphophonemic system, and lexicon), varieties of Street Setswana are all linked by the fact that they index the speaker's urbanness, an important part of people's identity as modern, fashionable South Africans (Cook 2002, see also Spitulnik 1998).

In addition to Street Setswana, there are also regional dialects of Setswana that vary significantly from the standard variety. Most Setswana speakers understand and speak Sesotho and Sepedi, as well, which are closely related to Setswana. These three languages are considered distinct languages rather than closely related dialects only because of the precolonial politics of European missionization. Nevertheless, they have been codified as separate languages for at least 150 years.

As with Setswana, there are numerous dialects of Afrikaans (including Tsotsitaal and regional dialects), Zulu (standard Zulu, urban Zulu, and Is'-camtho), Sesotho (standard Sesotho, Pretoria Sotho), and English spoken and/or heard in North West Province (Slabbert and Finlayson 2000). Not only are people multidialectal with regard to their "mother tongue," Setswana, then, but they may also command different dialects of the other languages in their repertoires.

Referring back to Ezra, Frances, Mr. Tau, and the Mmutles, then, these typical residents of Tlhabane township are all multilingual *and* multidialectal speakers. It is beyond the scope of this chapter to go into detail about how each of these individuals uses the particular languages and dialects in his or her repertoire to pursue their various life projects. It is sufficient to point out that each one of them has a sophisticated understanding of the social salience attached to using different styles of Street Setswana, to codeswitching between Setswana and English, and to incorporating lexical items from Afrikaans, Zulu, and Pedi into their speech, and that all of them deploy these interactional strategies on a daily basis. Perhaps a trivial reality in the lives of these people, these language behaviors seem quite remarkable in light of the language curriculum being taught in Tlhabane's schools.

Language in Education

Language policies in schools are rightly considered the heart of any national language policy. It is, after all, through the state-sponsored education system that most members of a society acquire literacy, knowledge of second and third languages, and information and attitudes about the "correct" form of the official language(s), and the relative status of the different languages they encounter (Kembo 2000, Bamgbose 1991). In South Africa, where a majority of children complete at least primary school, it follows that the language policies emanating from the Ministry of Education play a major role in shaping people's linguistic behavior and attitudes.

Although the South African constitution enshrines eleven official languages on a national level, what does this mean for language instruction in primary schools in Tlhabane? How does the current curriculum depart from the hated apartheid system that had children learning via the medium of their "home" language in primary school, but then switching to a mandatory 50/50 split between Afrikaans and English medium in secondary school?

Because Tlhabane was previously part of the Tswana "bantustan," government schools in and around Tlhabane abandoned the apartheid curriculum long before the new Constitution was written. As a quasi-independent nation, the Bophuthatswana had its own Department of Education, and was able to shift away from the apartheid regime's approach to the language of instruction back in the 1970s. This does not mean, as one might expect, that Bophuthatswana schools emphasized Setswana through high school, when the apartheid regime would have had them teaching in English and Afrikaans. Rather, English medium instruction was gradually introduced earlier and earlier, until by 1977, students studied Setswana as a subject until the end of secondary school, whereas all academic subjects were taught in English from Grade Four on (Bophuthatswana Department of Education 1977). This was due to popular pressure, in Bophuthatswana as elsewhere, from students and their parents to provide earlier access to English so that they might have a real chance to become proficient in the language of economic advancement. This system, as well as the pedagogical methods used to implement it, is still in place in ex-Bophuthatswana. In fact, since the fall of the "homeland" regime in 1994, it has been exported to the areas of North West Province that were not part of the Tswana "bantustan." In effect, then, the language policies in the "homeland" schools had already departed from apartheid policies by the time the new Constitution came into being, and the language situation in the schools has changed very little since 1994. Circa 1997, schools in Tlhabane still taught English, Afrikaans, and Setswana in the same proportions as before. Children in Tlhabane attend six years of primary school, three years of middle school, and three years of high school. When children enter the first grade (usually at age six or seven), they are taught exclusively in Setswana, presumed to be the "home language" for most. English is introduced unsystematically in the first grade, and then more formally in the second year. Afrikaans is introduced as a subject in the third grade, and by the fourth grade, most subjects are taught via the medium of English. Setswana remains a mandatory subject through grade twelve.

On an ideological level, then, the language policies in Tlhabane's schools anticipated Founding Provision Six (even as they hearken back to the apartheid era) in two important ways. First is the assumption that Setswana speakers don't (or don't need to) speak other African languages, and second, that there is only one legitimate form of Setswana. Thus, the language teachers in Tlhabane's schools actively police the boundaries between Setswana and other languages, as well as between "proper Setswana" and the forms they consider corrupt and inferior. In addition, given that most adults don't use standard Setswana in their everyday interactions, children from Tswana-speaking homes usually require remedial instruction in the standard form of the language. Students enter school not only with simplified grammar and limited vocabulary—a normal stage of language acquisition—but with a lot of non standard words that teachers seek to excise from their vocabulary. These range from words that are standard in "another" black South African language to words that are borrowed into Setswana from English and Afrikaans and "Setswanalized." Some examples of the "foreign" words I heard being banned from Setswana classrooms are:

Table 3.1:

Word (lang. of origin)	**English gloss**	**standard Setswana**
etsa (Sotho)	do	*dira*
mama/papa (Afrikaans/Sotho)	mother/father	*mme/ rre*
konomaka (Afrikaans)	clean	*phepafatsa*
kamore (Afrikaans)	room	*phaposi*
distories (English)	stories	*dikgang*
Krismas (English)	Christmas	*Botsalo jwa Morena*
dikwatlele (Afrikaans)	dishes	*dijana*

Most of these words have been used by Setswana speakers for generations, and are only considered "foreign" by language purists. Setswana teachers not only label these words "incorrect," but also feel they symbolize a dangerous trend toward abandoning or contaminating Setswana culture and identity (Kotze 2000). As teachers of "pure" Setswana, these professionals thus see themselves as ethnic nationalists fighting for the survival of their culture and identity. This perceived threat of linguistic and moral degeneration is revealed in the way teachers characterize lexical borrowing in Setswana. Mr. Tau, the primary school principal profiled above, refers to lexical borrowing as "stealing." At Sunnyside Primary School in Tlhabane, Mrs. Mmutle, the fifth-grade Setswana teacher, regards borrowing as laziness at best, cultural treason at worst. She carefully corrects her students as they give oral presentations, cautioning them to use *sejanaga* instead of *bese* (bus), *peretshitswana* instead of *baesekele* (bicycle), and *terena* instead of *sitimela* (train).[5] After class, I told her that I couldn't find *peretshitswana* in my Setswana-English dictionary. "What did they say for bicycle?" she asked. I said "*baesekele.*" Mrs. Mmutle replied, "No, they are being lazy! We are trying to phase out that language; we want to speak OUR language." It should be noted that most Setswana speakers consider terms like *sejanaga* and *peretshitswana* extremely arcane, and it would be very unusual, not to say ridiculous, to hear them in conversation.

While Setswana teachers don't readily acknowledge that standard Setswana is not the only form of spoken Setswana, they do so implicitly by calling this variety "pure Setswana" or "clean Setswana" (*Setswana se se phepa, Setswana se se tlhapileng*). Thus, the state-sponsored version of Setswana is considered not only linguistically correct, but also morally superior to other varieties. The need to distinguish between "pure Setswana" and some other (unnamed) variety is best exemplified in the Setswana portion of the national matriculation exam. Since at least 1994, the Department of Education has included a section on the test where students must provide the "pure Setswana" equivalents for a number of terms. In 1996, this section read as follows:

> *(g) Kwala mafoko a a latelang ka Setswana se se phepa*
> (Write the following words in pure Setswana)

i.	*Silabase*	("syllabus" from English)
ii.	*Sepitikopo*	("speed cop" from English)
iii.	*Tshampione*	("champion" from English)
iv.	*Ripoto*	("report" from English)
v.	*Sepatshe*	("wallet" from Afrikaans)

There are several striking observations to make about the language policies in the Tlhabane schools. First, and most obvious, is the fact that little has changed since 1994. If language is seen as one of the tools of democratization and making restitution for the evils of apartheid, it is unclear how the Ministry of Education, which is in charge of language policies in schools, intends to approach those tasks. Second, the teaching of Setswana, English, and Afrikaans perpetuates a system in which Setswana is considered the "home language" and English and Afrikaans are taught as "languages of wider communication." Although we saw above that many Setswana speakers also command two or three other "historically disadvantaged" South African languages, this is clearly not the result of having learned them in school. Finally, the school language policies overlook the issue of multidialectalism altogether. Standard Setswana, despite its lack of real usefulness in everyday life, is taught as though it were the only variety of Setswana. Urban varieties and even the more "respectable" regional varieties are derided, corrected, and marked "wrong" on national exams.

The rationale for this configuration of language subjects and media of instruction in the schools in North West is the presumption that most students speak Setswana as their home language, that they need (and want) competence in English for social and economic reasons, and that Afrikaans still plays a significant (if unpopular) role in the region's economy and demographics. Many teachers speak of "phasing out" Afrikaans gradually, but they are aware of the strong sensitivities surrounding this issue.

What is the effect, then, of a language curriculum that presumes a population of ethnic Tswanas who (1) speak a single, standard dialect of Setswana as their home language, (2) require English as a vehicle for participating in the national and international economy, (3) must endure obligatory Afrikaans lessons because "the language of apartheid" still has a role to play in the region, and (4) do not need to speak other African languages? In a community of multilingual and multidialectal individuals who have very little practical use for the standard version of their "mother tongue," these policies serve to symbolically silence the realities of their lives. Policing the boundary between standard Setswana and Street Setswana through admonishment, correction, and testing may reinforce people's attitudes that standard Setswana is an important symbol of their ethnic identity, but it does not change the way they communicate outside the classroom. Similarly, failing to offer instruction in Zulu, Xhosa, Pedi, or Tsonga to students in the North West may enable Tswana students to maintain their allegiance to a form of ethnolinguistic nationalism based on chauvinistic notions of separatism and superiority, but it does not change the importance or status of these other languages in people's everyday behavior or attitudes.

Susan Gal and Judith Irvine define "erasure" as "the process in which ideology, in simplifying the field of linguistic practices, renders some persons or activities or sociolinguistic phenomena invisible" (Gal and Irvine 1995). By this process of erasure, then—the ideological eclipsing of certain realities—the language ideologies that dominate official policy making, in particular the one culture/one language idea, obscure the dynamic multilingualism and multidialectalism that characterize the speech behaviors in this region. Gal and Irvine point out that erasure on the level of representation does not necessarily mean the "actual eradication of the awkward element," i.e., the behavior or phenomenon that doesn't fit into the official picture. This only becomes an issue when the "problematic" behavior becomes integral to some alternative ideology that might challenge the dominant notion of how things are/should be. For the time being in North West Province, the ideological erasure of individual multilingualism and multidialectalism does not seem to have much of a direct impact on people's behavior. On the other hand, it does provide the logic for policies that emphasize diversity (separateness) at the expense of unity (oneness), and rationalizes the allocation of resources based on an inaccurate picture of the linguistic repertoires that children bring to the classroom.

Language policy makers are not unaware of these contradictions, but seem powerless to address them. Makena E. Makapan, "Chief Language Practitioner" for Setswana in the Department of Arts, Culture, Science and Technology, acknowledges the challenges faced by those in language planning fields who are charged with promoting languages such as standard Setswana that are not necessarily the dominant spoken forms.[6] I asked him whether he thinks it is true that standard Setswana is dying out. He said yes, but added that the responsibility lies with parents, teachers, and government people to ensure that it doesn't, lest people lose their culture and identity. This may suggest some perception of an ideological threat to the idea of ethnolinguistic nationalism. When I noted that many Tswana-speaking parents choose to send their children to English-medium schools because they want their children to be able to compete on the job market, he agreed, but said that learning English doesn't have to mean forgetting Setswana, by which of course he means the standard dialect. Those on the front lines of the battle for linguistic and cultural purity (e.g. Setswana teachers) also appreciate the contradictions inherent in their work. Upwardly mobile educators send their children to English-medium schools, and wouldn't be caught dead using standard Setswana in their verbal interactions, preferring instead to use English or Street Setswana to index their modern, urban South Africanness. These are the very people trying to ensure that students appreciate the "proper" form of their mother tongue, standard Setswana. Meanwhile, English is competing for people's allegiance as the language of economic mobility; Afrikaans still plays a surprisingly important role in black popular culture and certain economic spheres; and Street Setswana is the everyday speech form of choice for most Tswanas. So while multilingualism and multidialectalism are being "erased" at the official level, they are thriving on the level of practice.

Language Policies in Broadcasting

South Africa's TV and radio stations' approach to language is an important component of the overall language policy picture for several reasons. First, like the schools, the broadcast media are not bound by the mandates of the South African Languages Bill. That is, while the Constitutional Provisions concerning language apply throughout society, the specific policy recommendations proposed by the Bill explicitly exclude both public and private broadcasters. Second, the broadcast media are one of the most important ways that people gain access to information *via* language, as well as gaining information *about* language (Fardon and Furniss 2000). Third, radio and TV are primarily oral, as opposed to written, media, a fact that has important implications for the ways that a multilingual society can be addressed and represented.

Although broadcasters are not bound by the proposed initiatives of the Languages Bill, the appropriate role of TV and radio in redressing the linguistic inequalities in South Africa has been the subject of serious debate since 1994. The South African Broadcasting Corporation, the country's public television broadcaster, set out to reorganize its programming schedule in February 1996 in order to comply with the eleven official languages mandate of the Constitution. The resulting line up featured one channel that broadcast programs in English, Zulu, Xhosa, Sindebele, and Seswati, a second channel featuring programs in English, Afrikaans, Setswana, Sepedi, Sesotho, Xitsonga, and Tshivenda, and a third channel broadcasting programs exclusively in English. Although the overwhelming proportion of prime-time programs were in English, the second most frequent language for prime-time programming was listed as "multilingual." This label applies to programs that feature dialogue characterized by code-switching or by hybrid dialects such as Pretoria Sotho or Street Setswana.

A night of TV programs from a May 2005 program guide reflects this same approach to language content, even if many of the individual programs have changed since 1996: SABC 1 features "That's So Raven" (from the U.S.) at 7:00, the news in Zulu at 7:30, "Generations," a South African made, multilingual drama series, at 8:00, and "Girlfriends" (from the U.S.) at 8:30. The line up on SABC 2 features programming in Afrikaans, English, and Sesotho, and SAABC 3 is all in English, including both local and American content.

With reference to the official ideological preoccupation with ethnolinguistic unity, then, the language policies of the SABC do not, in fact, erase multilingualism and multidialectalism the way the schools do. On the contrary, although SABC nods to the Constitution by attempting to offer at least some programming in each of the eleven official languages chiefly through its news broadcasts, the habits and preferences of the viewing public seem to play an important role in determining the proportions of English language programs to programs in other languages, and of "multilingual" programs to monolingual programs. In contrast to language learning in schools, broadcasting is an almost exclusively oral medium.[7] Because language purism most often reaches the heights of its prescriptiveness with regard to the written form, this may help explain why the idea of ethnolinguistic nationalism comes across more strongly in the classroom than on TV and radio.

Radio has undergone a similar transformation since the end of apartheid, and reflects a similarly relaxed approach to language/ethnic purity, as compared with that in the schools. In 1995, the Independent Broadcasting Authority, the umbrella agency that has oversight of all broadcasting in South Africa, began issuing radio licenses to community stations throughout South Africa (Minnie 2000). No longer controlled by the apartheid state, the airwaves were suddenly full of "local content," including all eleven official languages, and plenty more besides. The new radio stations in Gauteng, the Province that includes the major cities Johannesburg and Pretoria, include "ALX FM," "a talk and music station aimed at the Alexandra community in English, plus Nguni and Sotho languages, including Tsotsitaal" (Mail and Guardian newspaper, August 11-17 1995); and Radio TNT, "aimed at young people; broadcast by Technikon Northern Transvaal students in English, Tsonga, Venda, Zulu, North Sotho, and Tswana for 18 hours a day" (ibid.)

South Africa has a vibrant music industry, and there is therefore no shortage of "local content" to broadcast on radio. This stands in contrast to the TV broadcasters, who struggle to find quality South African-made TV programs. Although there were radio stations dedicated to the various language communities in South Africa before the end of apartheid, they did not necessarily program in indigenous languages. A survey of "local content" on various radio stations in 1995 found that "Setswana Stereo," for example, broadcast local content somewhere between 19 and 55 percent of its on-air time. The official radio station of Bophuthatswana, "Radio Bop," broadcast locally made music and programs only about 5 percent of the time.

In Tlhabane, many people previously listened to Radio Bop, which broadcast in Setswana and English, until Radio Mafisa came along in 1997. This hipper, more urban oriented local radio station began broadcasting a wide range of music, talk, and other formats, including a lot of Kwaito, the enormously popular urban black South African music, akin to hip hop in the U.S. Radio Mafisa's disc jockeys speak Street Setswana, Afrikaans, and English. Radio Mafisa quickly overtook Radio Bop as the station of choice in the urban and peri-urban areas around Tlhabane.

Exclusively oral, unfettered by presumptions that ethnic Tswanas only speak standard Setswana (and English for certain formal purposes), the radio stations in North West increasingly reflect lived linguistic practice, rather than an ideologically based ideal.

Conclusion

In practice the vast majority of black South Africans are both multilingual and multidialectal. Ethnic Tswanas in North West Province are but one example of a socially and historically constructed grouping that is to a large degree emblemized by the "pure" form of the language they are presumed to speak. Although the notion of linguistic, cultural and territorial unity has its roots in eighteenth-century Europe, it remains as powerful today as it was when it served as the basis for establishing the bantustans during the apartheid era. The prevalence and hegemonic nature of this idea is obvious in Founding Provision Six of the new Constitution. The celebrated document that boasts radical new freedoms and protections for South Africans of every racial, religious, sexual, and geographic community establishes eleven official languages (hence ethnic groupings) based on the same understanding of the relationship of linguistic practice to social and cultural belief that has been around for over two hundred years. What gets "erased" in the process are the very realities that distinguish life in South Africa for most blacks today. Their verbal interactions are governed not by the standard form of their "own" ethnic languages, but by the stylistic and strategic deployment of numerous language varieties. Explained away by language purists as "laziness" or the result of too much contact with "foreigners," the prevalence of individual multilingualism and multidialectalism may not constitute an immediate threat to those in power who would prefer to maintain the conventional cultural map of South Africa. But if a vision of South African unity based on pan-urban experience, or trans-ethnic identity were to take hold (as some expected it would under the leadership of the ANC), such behaviors would surely be increasingly scrutinized and vilified as a threat to the moral and philosophical foundations of the South African nation. Semi-

otic erasure would turn into practical action to address the "problem," and a great many South Africans would be surprised to learn that their everyday speech patterns have "suddenly" become a threat to the age-old myth of homogenous, bounded ethnic groups.

Notes

1. I am indebted to my students in Anthropology 260 at the University of Pretoria for their feedback on this chapter. Also to Alexis Arieff and Holiness Thebyane for their invaluable contributions.
2. The eleven official languages are: isiZulu, isiXhosa, siSwati, isiNdebele, Setswana, Sesotho, Sepedi, Tshivenda, Xitsonga, English, and Afrikaans.
3. Data for this study was gathered in 1996 and 1997.
4. All names in this section are pseudonyms.
5. Ironically, both *terena* and *sitimela* derive from English (from "train" and "steam").
6. Interview with Makapan on August 11, 1997.
7. The recent addition of English subtitles to many of the "multilingual" programs on SABC television is an interesting exception, and merits further analysis.

References Cited

Adendorff, R. 1995. "Fanakalo in South Africa." In *Language and Social History: Studies in South African Sociolinguistics.* R. Mesthrie, ed. Cape Town: David Philip.

Bamgbose, Ayo. 1991. "Language and Education," in *Language and the Nation: The Language Question in Sub-Saharan Africa.* Edinburgh: Edinburgh University Press., 62-108.

Black Sash. 1990. *Grasping the Prickly Pear: The Bophuthatswana Story.* [South Africa]: Black Sash.

Bophuthatswana Department of Education. 1977. *Annual Report of 1977.* Mafikeng.

Breutz, P. L. 1953. *The Tribes of Rustenburg and Pilansberg Districts.* Pretoria: The Government Printer.

Comaroff, Jean and John Comaroff. 1991. *Of Revelation and Revolution: Christianity, Colonialism and Consciousness in South Africa.* Chicago: Chicago University Press.

Cook, S.E. 1999. *Street Setswana: Language, Ideology and Identity in Post-Apartheid South Africa.* Ann Arbor: UMI Dissertations.

_____ 2002. "Urban Language in a Rural Setting: The Case of Phokeng, South Africa." In *Urban Life: Readings in the Anthropology of the City, 4th Edition.* George Gmelch and W.P. Zenner, eds. Prospect Heights, Il.: Waveland Press.

Fabian, Johannes. 1986. *Language and Colonial power: The Appropriation of Swahili in the Former Belgian Congo.* Cambridge, UK: Cambridge University Press.

Fardon, Richard and Graham Furniss. 2000. *African Broadcast Cultures: Radio in Transition.* Oxford: James Currey.

Gal, Susan and Judith Irvine. 1995. "The Boundaries of Languages and Disciplines: How Ideologies Construct Difference." *Social Research* 62.4: 967-1001.

Government of South Africa. 2003. South African Languages Bill. (Revised Final Draft April 2003).

Harries, Patrick. 1988. "The Roots of Ethnicity: Discourse and the Politics of Language Construction in South-East Africa." *African Affairs* 86(346): 25-52.

Herder, Johann G. 1966. "Essay on the Origin of Language." In *On the Origin of Language."* J. Moran transl., 85-166. New York: F. Ungar.

Humboldt, Wilhelm von. 1988. *On Language: The Diversity of Human Language-Structure and Its Influence on the Mental Development of Mankind.* Peter Heath, transl. Cambridge: Cambridge University Press.

Janson, T. and J. Tsonope. 1991. *Birth of a National Language: the History of Setswana.* Garborone: Heinemann Botswana.

Kembo, Jane. 2000. "Language in Education and Language Learning in Africa." In *African Voices,* Vic Webb and Kembo-Sure, eds. Cape Town: Oxford University Press.

Kotze, E. F. 1999. "Sociocultural and Linguistic Corollaries of Ethnicity in South African Society." *International Journal of the Sociology of Language.* 144 (2000): 7-17.

Mail and Guardian newspaper, August 11-17 1995.

Makoni, S. 1996. "Language and Identities in Southern Africa." *In Ethnicity in Africa: Roots, Meaning, and Implications.* L. de la Gorgendiere, J.K. King, and S. Vaughan (eds.). Edinburgh: Centre of African Studies, University of Edinburgh.

Minnie, J. 2000. "The Growth of Independent Broadcasting in South Africa: Lessons for Africa?" In *African Broadcast Cultures: Radio in Transition.* R. Fardon and Graham Furniss eds. Cape Town: David Philip Publishers.

Moodie, T. D. 1975. *The Rise of Afrikanerdom: Power, Apartheid, and the Afrikaner Civil Religion.* Berkeley: The University of California Press.

Slabbert, S. and Rosalie Finlayson. 2000. "I'm a cleva!": the linguistic makeup of identity in a South African urban environment." *International Journal of the Sociology of Language.* 144 (2000): 119-135.

Spitulnik D. 1998. "The Language of the City: Town Bemba as Urban Hybridity." *Journal of Linguistic Anthropology* 8.1 June: 30-59.

Spitulnik, Debra. 2001. "The Social Circulation of Media Discourse and the Mediation of Communities." In *Linguistic Anthropology : A Reader.* Alessandro Duranti, ed. Oxford: Blackwell Publishers, Inc.

Swigart, Leigh. 2000. "The Limits of Legitimacy: Language Ideology and Shift in Contemporary Senegal." *Journal of Linguistic Anthropology* 10.1, June: 90-130.

Tambiah, Stanley J. 1996. "The Nation-State in Crisis and the Rise of Ethnonationalism." In *The Politics of Difference:Ethnic Premises in a World of Power.* Wilmsen, E.N. and Patrick McAllister, eds. Chicago: University of Chicago Press. Pp. 124-143.

Templin, J. Alton. 1984. *Ideology on a Frontier: The Theological Foundation of Afrikaner Nationalism, 1652-1910.* Wesport, CT: Greenwood Press.

Willan, B. 1996. *Sol Plaatje: Selected Writings.* Athens: Ohio University Press.

PART II

Silence and Power in Ethnographic Perspective

Chapter 4

Strategic Alterity and Silence in the Promotion of California's Proposition 187 and of the Confederate Battle Flag in South Carolina

Ann E. Kingsolver

White supremacist arguments that were used to support (1) the fear of increasing immigration from Latin America into California, which propelled voters' approval of California Proposition 187 in 1994, and (2) the display of the confederate battle flag on public property in South Carolina had this in common: both invoked neoliberal capitalist and U.S. constitutional rhetoric. California Proposition 187 has been ruled unconstitutional and the confederate battle flag was lowered from the dome of the South Carolina statehouse on 1 July, 2000, but the white supremacist logic that Mills (1997) has argued is embedded in "the racial contract" in the U.S.A. continues to be employed increasingly, perhaps, at a time of rising unemployment. This chapter takes up the question of how the term "freedom" has been used to silence experiences and articulations of inequality, in the logic and practice of both white supremacy and neoliberal capitalism.

Proposition 187, "Globalization," and Strategic Alterity: Marked and Unmarked Immigrants

In the fall of 1994, the same year that the neoliberal trade policy NAFTA went into effect, California voters received in our mailboxes the thick booklet of ballot initiatives to be decided in the November elections. Proposition 187 began with this statement:

> The People of California find and declare as follows:
> That they have suffered and are suffering economic hardship caused by the presence of illegal aliens in this state.
> That they have suffered and are suffering personal injury and damage caused by the criminal conduct of illegal aliens in this state.
> That they have a right to the protection of their government from any person or persons entering this country unlawfully.
>
> Therefore, the People of California declare their intention to provide for cooperation between their agencies of state and local government with the federal government, and to establish a system of required notification by and between such agencies to prevent illegal aliens in the United States from receiving benefits or public services in the State of California.

Proposition 187 galvanized public debate [in Mexico as well as in the U.S.] about who constituted the *public* in California.[1] Who was marked? Who was unmarked? What was strategic about that alterity in the language of Proposition 187, and how was it related to other social and political projects?

U.S. District Court Judge Mariana Pfaelzer ruled the bulk of the proposition unconstitutional in March 1998, and injunctions prevented its going into effect between its passage and the moment it was struck down. All along, the primary purpose of California Proposition 187 seemed to be symbolic, even to a principal proponent, Governor Pete Wilson (who was reelected on the same ballot as Prop. 187). In his only debate with gubernatorial challenger Kathleen Brown, Governor Wilson said that as soon as it was passed, Proposition 187 would be challenged by a lawsuit and taken to the U.S. Supreme Court. Kevin Johnson (1997: 178) provides strong evidence that Proposition 187 was advanced to support nativist ideology rather than to save the State of California money (as purported), since it would end up costing the state more to implement than it would save in cutting social services to the targeted population. The power of the ballot initiative seemed to be, then, in its service as a key symbol (Ortner 1973) in what Paul Farmer (1993) has called the geography of blame. Although the bill would have cut public services to *all* residents of California without legal immigration status, in the pre-electoral rhetoric supporting Proposition 187 (or the "Save Our State" initiative), only Latino undocumented residents were *marked* as the *racialized* enemies of the "People of California," who were, in turn, silently and powerfully *whitened* through what Omi and Winant (1994: 56) define as a *racial project*: "*simultaneously an interpretation, representation, or explanation of racial dynamics, and an effort to reorganize and redistribute resources along particular racial lines.*"

The conflation of nationality and racialization in images of "Mexican immigrants," and the assumed physical threat of permeated membranes of the U.S. national body, racialized—silently and confoundingly—as white, in pro-Prop. 187 rhetoric relied upon what Charles W. Mills (1997: 32-33) has called the "racial contract." He says:

> The whole point of establishing a moral hierarchy and juridically partitioning the polity according to race is to secure and legitimate the privileging of those individuals designated as white/persons and the exploitation of those individuals designated as nonwhite/subpersons.

The text of Proposition 187, and its supporters, while loudly proclaiming the danger to public welfare of those marked as "illegal aliens," was silently making another assertion even *more* powerfully: that the group named as the "sufferers" at the hands of those "illegal aliens" were the *true* People of California: a stable, unified, white public. I invoke "white" here as a symbolic category, not a biological one. The distinction "Californian"/"other" indexed other registered distinctions (Foucault 1979: 220) like white/nonwhite, even though voters on Proposition 187 could not be racialized uniformly parallel to their support or opposition. At issue here was just who comprised "the People of California," and who was speaking for them in this text. California Proposition 187 was one of several legislative attempts in the U.S.A. to limit access of noncitizens to public services and to restrict citizenship (cf. Ono and Sloop 2002, and the 2004 passage of Arizona Proposition 200). As Richard Delgado (1999: 251) has put it, and as is clear from the language of Proposition 187's introduction, "efforts to limit citizenship are efforts to maintain a system of white supremacy and to give that system the veneer of fairness and principle." And as Renato Rosaldo (1999: 257), in a discussion of cultural citizenship, said, "in California statewide initiatives provide citizens with an occasion for voting their prejudices. Proposition 187 was arguably in large measure an expression of white supremacy." R. Michael Alvarez and Tara L. Butterfield (2000), political scientists, used the Voter News Service exit polls to interpret why the 59 percent of California's voters who passed Proposition 187 voted for it; they concluded that the passage of Prop. 187 was linked with "cyclical nativism" related to a poor economy and with endorsement of the policy by gubernatorial and senate candidates, who often used stereotypical images of immigrants in their campaign ads.

It is the largely silent yet powerful assertion of the "People of California" [in the language of Proposition 187] as a stable, unified, symbolically privileged public that I want to examine next, with the inspiration of Mexican political cartoonists. Just days before the election in California in which Proposition 187 was passed and Governor Wilson was reelected, Mexican political cartoonists—who are free to engage in Geertzian (1977) deep play with political notions so often left unnamed in the public sphere—were comparing Governor Wilson and other Proposition 187 supporters to Nazis and the KKK. In one example from 29 October, 1994, sharing the front page of *El Día* with the announcement of a Mexican boycott of U.S. products and a report of California police injuring a high school student at a protest of Proposition 187 in Los Angeles, a cartooned white supremacist—wearing the hood of a KKK member and a Nazi armband—says, "We are also getting ready for a rally in support of 187." The character, drawn by political cartoonist Terrazas, is painting a sign supporting Pete Wilson.

The political cartoonists in Mexico, and some in the U.S., could state publicly what was silenced in so many ways in the U.S.: that there was white supremacist support for Proposition 187, specifically through the organization named FAIR, the Federation for American Immigration Reform, which received funding from the Pioneer Fund, a eugenicist (and many would argue, by extension, a white supremacist) organization.[2] Jean Stefancic (1997) documented the links between the Pioneer Fund, FAIR, and Proposition 187 supporters. White supremacist organizations have also, of course, backed other anti-immigrant legislation and English-only initiatives. The links between dollars going to specifically white supremacist causes and the anti-immigrant publicity are hard to trace, though, and rarely are they publicly announced. Disguised as populist groundswells, such targeted campaigns often appear and disappear in ways that seem a bit mysterious to those not funding them.

Between the passage of Proposition 187 and its being declared unconstitutional, I moved from California to South Carolina. In the spring of

2000, as John McCain, George W. Bush, and other Republican contenders for the presidential nomination moved into South Carolina and worked the state before the primary vote, Project USA anti-immigration billboards went up around the state, and there were anti-immigrant television advertisements. The ads stopped and the billboard signs made way for Chick-Fil-A's misspelling cows as soon as Bush had won the primary. How did anti-immigrant propaganda get read differently in the social landscape of South Carolina than in California? Was the racial contract that propelled the passage of California Proposition 187 the same racial contract that sanctioned anti-immigrant billboards and pro-confederate flag demonstrations in South Carolina? I will move to a discussion of silencing and the confederate battle flag in the next section, but first I want to contextualize anti-immigrant rhetoric in the U.S.A. in reference to the matrix of events and processes glossed as "globalization." This has, of course, been especially marked in the national climate since 11 September, 2001.

Patricia Zavella wrote this about the racialized atmosphere in which Proposition 187 was passed in California:

> The new nativism we see in California—expressed through the attempt to pass the English-Only proposition, and more recently the passage of Proposition 187 and the introduction of the California Civil Rights Initiative [Proposition 209, which would eliminate Affirmative Action policies in California]—reflects a sense of loss of white control over the affairs of state.... What is new about the fin de siècle nativism is that white supremacy has been undermined by global economic restructuring, which has created tremendous wealth while increasing the vulnerability of white citizens....
>
> (Zavella 1997: 136-137)

I agree with Zavella and others that white supremacist politics have to be seen in relation to global capitalism. As bell hooks (2000: vii) has written, "As a nation we are afraid to have a dialogue about class even though the ever-widening gap between rich and poor has already set the stage for ongoing and sustained class warfare." The silence about class is supplanted by race-talk in what I think of as a process of strategic alterity in the logic of capitalism—particularly the language game of neoliberal capitalism, in which "citizens" are free to trade in the world market, and strategically "othered" noncitizens of the market are busy reproducing those free-trading citizens. Anti-immigrant talk in the U.S. is often about class. Examples range from the passage of the Chinese Exclusion Act in 1882 (Frank

1999:74) to post-9/11 immigration reforms (cf. Balibar 1999 on class racism and Ong 1999 on the production of cultural citizens).

The inability to discuss class inequities in the U.S., in part because of their blatant contradictions of U.S. Constitutional rhetoric of equality, has been noted by observers of U.S. culture from deTocqueville on. As Sherry Ortner (1991: 164) put it, "class is central to American social life, but it is rarely spoken in its own right. Rather, it is represented through other categories of social difference: gender, ethnicity, race, and so forth." Tomás Almaguer (1994) has documented the development of the ideological categories of "free white labor" / "unfree nonwhite labor" in the history of the state of California, with Native Americans, Mexicans, and Asian immigrants variously invoked in white-dominated discourse as somehow "unfairly competing with and fettering white labor" (Almaguer 1994:15) in a racialized and class-based symbolic system meant to justify white antipathy toward "nonwhite" groups.

As Mary Douglas (1986) would note, reinforcing such symbolic categories as "free"/ "unfree" and "white"/ "nonwhite" requires selective remembering and forgetting. At the time that Proposition 187 was proposed, nearly a year into implementation of the neoliberal North American Free Trade Agreement, there was quite an effort at selective remembering, or marking, involved in its supporters' discussion of terms like "Mexican" or "immigrant." "Mexican" was used as a code to index not simply a nationality but also a class position, a gender identity, and a racialized identity. The stereotyped "Mexican" male working-class laborer invoked in political cartoons related to NAFTA, in fearful representations of a "leaky" border, and in so many other sources relied on selective forgetting of the range in class, gender, age, and citizenship status of those identified as "Mexican." The process of racialization always implies selective remembering and forgetting of specific attributes and attaching them to power, and in Proposition 187, further forgetting was necessary in order to codify "immigrants" as Mexican when in 1994 people came from *many* countries into California.

The stereotypes promoted through the support and passage of California Proposition 187 were not merely annoying or misleading; they were very, very dangerous. Hate crimes against Latinos increased sharply after the passage of Proposition 187 (Finnigan 1995: 6). Since it is impossible to tell citizenship by looking at a person, the discrimination affected citizens and noncitizens alike. The pro-187 advertisements portrayed a California being overrun by undocumented Latinos. The largest concentration of undocumented Latinos is in Los Angeles County, according to

Rodriguez (1996: 18), and in that county, 80 to 85 percent of foreign-born Latinos are U.S. citizens. The Coalition for Humane Immigrant Rights of Los Angeles documented the increase in incidences of hate crimes and other acts of discrimination against Latinos in the period following the passage of California Proposition 187, aimed against citizens of the U.S. and of other nations alike, based on visual marking of individuals as "the other." Many of these experiences of discrimination were specifically racialized. A Latina mother (with U.S. citizenship) and her children, for example, were told by their apartment complex manager that they could not use the pool after 6:00 p.m. because in the evenings it was "for whites only" (Finnigan 1995: 6). Another U.S. citizen, a Latina, was turned away from a hospital while she was hemorrhaging. She was told that the hospital no longer treated Hispanics. As a result, she lost her baby (Martinez 1995: 18). The Coalition for Humane Immigrant Rights of Los Angeles reported many more examples, often violent, of empowered hatred against visually targeted Latinos in California following the passage of Proposition 187. These acts, especially when carried out or sanctioned by police officers representing the state (regardless of their own identities), seemed to support a white supremacist notion of who constituted the public of, or who had a right to citizenship in, California and the U.S.A. The Federation for American Immigration Reform (2004), while campaigning for Arizona's Proposition 200 (a corollary to California's Proposition 187 that was passed in 2004), claimed that the initiative would decrease discrimination because services would only be denied after identity papers had been checked. The question here is whose papers get checked and whose do not, and what violations of human rights might take place before the issue of papers is even raised.

Strategic silences are used by the organizations that supported Proposition 187. For example, on the website of FAIR (Federation for American Immigration Reform 2005), a major backer of Proposition 187, there is a page listing a chronology of terrorist attacks in the U.S. from 1990 through 2001. The page appears to be intended to fuel anti-immigrant sentiments; in the year 2000, the chronology on that page did not list what, at that time, was the attack with the most fatalities: the bombing in Oklahoma City by a U.S. citizen. Through being silent about terrorist acts carried out by individuals identifying as white and Christian, the website's authors would seem to be equating "terrorist" unproblematically with strategically othered immigrants.

What does silence mean, politically? Project USA, the organization sponsoring the anti-immigration billboard in South Carolina mentioned above, claimed to have been silenced in 1999 when public pressure in New York City led to a billboard company asking to be released from a contract with Project USA to display a similar anti-immigration advertisement. Project USA staff, on a version of the organization's website (Project USA), asked this question:

> How can it be inciting hate to state the facts about immigration numbers?.... The words 'racist' and 'hate' have become tantamount to the word 'communist' in the 1950s. The PC crowd has achieved an autocratic silence of which Joe McCarthy could only have dreamed.

Were residents of New York City silencing Project USA when they spoke up about not wanting to see anti-immigration rhetoric on that billboard? What are the implications of *not* speaking up? How do U.S. residents become complicit with white supremacist claims by remaining silent about hate crimes and other forms of discrimination based on strategic alterity? Richard Butler, leader of the Aryan Nations compound in Coeur d'Alene, Idaho, said the following to an interviewer in a KSPS television documentary (Bowers 2000). When the interviewer asked about public support for a whites-only movement, "Silence is acceptance?", Butler responded, "Oh, absolutely."

Divergent Views of Silence and Freedom

On the morning that I began writing this, I was in the grocery store parking lot and happened to glance up as the man getting into the car facing mine reached out his arm to close his car door. I saw a spiderweb tattooed around his elbow, and a five-inch swastika on his forearm below it. My partner, a news omnivore, tells me that the spiderweb tattoo signifies for white supremacists the killing of an African American. I do not know if this is what the man intended to tell the world in this silent act of body alteration, but along with the confederate flag struggle in South Carolina it has made me think about the many ways in which white supremacist claims are made silently in public space and how that silence facilitates public tolerance of emphatic intolerance.

Some people think of white supremacist views as comfortably regionalized in the U.S.; that may be the way that many interpreted international reporting on the confederate flag debate in South Carolina. Certainly, there are overt signs of white supremacist views in the state. For example,

when I was driving around rural South Carolina with my family, looking for a place to live, I saw one yard with these lawn ornaments: the ubiquitous wooden woman bent over showing her polka-dotted bloomers, a jumping frog, a plaque with the Christian serenity prayer, and a life-size lawn gnome in full KKK regalia. Such public signs are very frightening, and sadly they are prevalent in every region of the U.S.A. For example, Kathleen Blee, who has studied Ku Klux Klan participants across the U.S., reports (personal communication, 1996) that the largest KKK chapter is in the Santa Cruz mountains in California.

Returning to the spiderweb and swastika tattoo, how is that tattoo incommensurate with other signs we exhibit in the public sphere? I suppose a large movement of U.S. residents with inclusive and nonviolent philosophies and peace sign tattoos could be perceived as threatening to some; certainly the Project USA website claimed that multiculturalists were as silencing and oppressive as McCarthyism. But is it an equivalent threat to the silent, strategically altering, life-threatening sign language of swastikas and, sometimes, confederate flags? I think not. Neither did the American Civil Liberties Union (ACLU) representative who told Project USA members that they had no case with regard to getting their billboard sign put back up in New York.[3]

Many, from ethicists to jurists to activists, have thought hard about the line between Constitutionally-guaranteed freedom of speech and the agency of spoken or unspoken messages in inspiring violent acts. In the question/answer section of an ACLU briefing paper on hate speech (American Civil Liberties Union), the question, "What about nonverbal symbols, like swastikas and burning crosses: are they constitutionally protected?" was raised and given this response:

> Symbols of hate are constitutionally protected if they're worn or displayed before a general audience in a public place—say, in a march or at a rally in a public park. But the First Amendment doesn't protect the use of nonverbal symbols to encroach upon, or desecrate, private property, such as burning a cross on someone's lawn or spray-painting a swastika on the wall of a synagogue or dorm.
>
> In its 1992 decision in *R.A.V. v. St. Paul*, the Supreme Court struck down as unconstitutional a city ordinance that prohibited cross-burnings based on their symbolism, which the ordinance said makes many people feel "anger, alarm or resentment." Instead of prosecuting the cross-burner for the content of his act, the city government could have rightfully tried him under criminal trespass and/or harassment laws.
>
> The Supreme Court has ruled that symbolic expression, whether swastikas, burning crosses or, for that matter, peace signs, is protected by the First Amend-

> ment because it's "closely akin to 'pure speech.'" That phrase comes from a landmark 1969 decision in which the Court held that public school students could wear black armbands in school to protest the VietNam War. And in another landmark ruling, in 1989, the Court upheld the right of an individual to burn the American flag in public as a symbolic expression of disagreement with government policies.

Does the confederate battle flag constitute a symbolic code of "pure speech" that can be read in one sense as inspiring or celebrating violent acts—specifically, white supremacist hate crimes—but which cannot be legislated against because of its literal silence? This is one of the questions that have been at the core of the debate about whether to fly or retire the flag over public buildings in the southeastern U.S. at the turn of this century.[4]

At the risk of overly simplifying a long and complex struggle, I will summarize here a few moments in the symbolic and physical contestation in South Carolina over what it means to fly the Confederate battle flag over the statehouse, and where it may or may not be flown. I think this debate about the confederate battle flag is an example of how arguments about who is entitled to full citizenship in the public sphere and who is not can be made symbolically, powerfully, and in *complete silence.* In the spring of 1997, I attended a ceremony marking the reopening of the South Carolina statehouse, which had been closed for renovation for several years, to see who might attend, seeing the statehouse as *their* statehouse. Mostly, there were the legislators who had authorized the renovations. Miss South Carolina sang. It looked to me more like a private party than a public event, and state troopers at least *appeared* to be protecting numerous confederate battle flag supporters from two young protestors holding a sign that said Take It Down, as they stood between them. In January 2000, I attended a very different event at the statehouse. Nearly fifty thousand people demonstrated, calling for the confederate battle flag to come down from atop the statehouse. In response to the pro-flag campaign slogan claiming that the flag represented Heritage, Not Hate, another slogan (widely represented on signs that day) was, "Your heritage is my slavery." Lori Donath (2002) has demonstrated, from a linguistic perspective, the link between public discursive claims to "Southern" history and heritage and "white" identity.

Support for flying over the statehouse the confederate battle flag, which has been there only since 1962[5]—directly linked to civil rights struggles in the state and nation—was politically if not numerically strong. The last governor, Republican David Beasley, after announcing that he had been told by God at 3:00 A.M. to bring the flag down, lost support within his own party, and his successor, Democratic Governor Jim Hodges, won in a campaign in which the flag figured in such Republican and coalition ads as "Dump Beasley; keep the flag." In the spring session of the South Carolina legislature, there was a prolonged debate about whether, and where, to move the flag. This ended in a "compromise" which moved the confederate battle flag to the lawn of the statehouse, on Main Street, behind a tall monument to a confederate soldier. On 1 July, 2000, the day that the flag was lowered from the flagpole on top of the statehouse and raised in front of the statehouse, there were two gatherings segregated by a strong showing of state police: one on the south side of the statehouse from which only the lowering could be seen, and one on the north side of the statehouse, from which both the lowering and the raising could be seen. Protestors of the flag's continued presence on statehouse grounds moved down Main Street in complete silence—paralleling the silent power the confederate battle flag has as a symbol of exclusion.

Here is one example of how the symbolic struggle has continued. Maurice Bessinger is the owner of a local restaurant chain in South Carolina called Maurice's Barbecue. He is known for, among other things, challenging the 1964 Civil Rights Act at the level of the Supreme Court (a case he lost) and for the array of Christian and pro-confederate cause literature and clothing available, along with the barbecue hash, in his restaurants. After the confederate battle flag came down from the statehouse, very large confederate battle flags went up on poles in front of all Maurice's Barbecue restaurants, flown with the South Carolina flag but in the absence of the American flag (in symbolic support of "states' rights" and disapproval of national Civil Rights legislation—see Bessinger 2005 for his political views). Since then, Maurice Bessinger was first fined for erecting an unauthorized sign, then the fine was reduced, and finally the ordinance was changed to allow the flying of a smaller version of the confederate battle flag in front of businesses. Then, in turn, Wal-Mart, Winn-Dixie, Kroger, and the Piggly Wiggly grocery chains made the decision to take Maurice's Barbecue products off their shelves.

There were numerous letters to the editors of regional newspapers from those articulating various positions about the meaning of the public use of the confederate battle flag. Maurice Bessinger wrote an editorial in *The State* newspaper comparing his oppression in having rocks thrown through the windows of his restaurants to oppression of the Jews in Germany, in

"Crystal Night," as he wrote it. One of his supporters, Tony Dillard, wrote in to the same paper (27 September, 2000):

> It now appears that other stores are jumping on the bandwagon to remove Maurice's BBQ sauce from their shelves. I believe this is being done as a knee-jerk reaction to the racial views held by Maurice Bessinger.
>
> Should the owner or chairperson of every company be publicly profiled to see if their racial, religious and political ideology meet popular public opinion?

In the fall of 2000, Lonnie Randolph, a spokesperson for the NAACP in South Carolina, stated (personal communication) that it might be very helpful if more people like Maurice Bessinger would fly the confederate battle flag outside their businesses: grocery stores, dental offices, hospitals, travel and insurance agencies, and so on. This way, consumers would know where they stood and would be able to make the decision to boycott those businesses. The NAACP has sustained an economic boycott of the state of South Carolina over the confederate flag issue that kept $30 million in tourism and conference revenues out of the state in 1999 and 2000 (UPI); the boycott was reaffirmed in 2004 (NAACP 2004).

It is the unmarked, or silent agreement with discriminatory policies that is most harmful to the public. One public-owned utility acted by this logic when its employees were forbidden from using Piggie Park parking lots for vehicles carrying the company logo unless the driver was making a service call on the building itself (Staples 2002:A16).[6] Carrie Crenshaw (1997) argues that it is vital to expose the silence about assertions linking whiteness and power in political discourse, as a step forward in addressing racism in U.S. public life. Projects attempting to do that have been documented by Papa and Lassiter (2003) and Schramm-Pate and Lussier (2003).

I think it is worth noting, here, the power that symbols have *because* of their multivalent meanings, as Victor Turner (1970) and others have pointed out. Maurice Bessinger put up Whites Only signs at his restaurant in the 1950s and 1960s, and legislation forced him to remove those words – and to cease enforcing them by standing at the door of his restaurant with a baseball bat. His recent practice of flying the confederate battle flag in front of his restaurants could be interpreted, and is by many, as another Whites Only sign; but because it is not expressed in words, it has proven nearly impossible to address through legislation. Not only are discriminatory symbols supposed to be tolerated by all South Carolinians who pass by (on a road, by the way, long named the Jefferson Davis highway but marked—since the flag came off the statehouse—with brand-new flags of the confederacy), but there is another kind of deep play going on: not only a game of "capture the flag" but a game of "capture the meaning" of the words *free speech*, and a strange interpretation of free-market capitalism. After the grocery stores, including one WalMart Superstore that is directly across the Jefferson Davis Highway, or U.S. Route 1, from a Maurice's Barbecue, pulled Maurice's sauce from their shelves, picketers began to appear with signs saying Wal-Mart Is Racist, "Bessinger's attorney has asked Attorney General Charlie Condon to bring an unfair trade practices action against Wal-Mart, BiLo, Food Lion, Harris Teeter, Kroger, Piggly Wiggly, Publix, Sam's Club and Winn-Dixie for locking out his products" (*Lexington County Chronicle* 11/2/00). Maurice Bessinger hosted Reform Party Vice Presidential candidate Ezola Foster at his Piggy Park barbecue restaurant in West Columbia on 24 October, 2000. She said at a press conference there that the food retailers were "'hypocrites' for abridging freedom of speech" (*Lexington County Chronicle* 10/26/00). How can the public's not buying Maurice Bessinger's barbecue sauce be interpreted as a violation of his free speech? This claim to silencing, especially the claim to be violated like Jewish Germans were on Kristallnacht, is an inversion reminiscent of the culture of terror (Taussig 1987) and the strategies of silencing associated with it. Freedom of speech has itself become a multivalent symbol.

Conclusions

Strategic alterity, or the shifting, selective marking of an "other" in order to limit access to symbolic and material resources by members of that marked group, is a strategy which serves neoliberal capitalism in that there are always marked groups, whose citizenship is somehow questioned, laboring to produce what the free-trading marketeers, citizens of the global market, sell. The free-marketeers are often read as white, and benefit from the "racial contract." So much has to be forgotten, silenced, or masked to rationalize a meritocracy. As economic inequality becomes even greater, the silence about class differences is resounding, as is the silence about the process of strategic alterity that serves the class divide. The use of the word freedom in neoliberal capitalist rhetoric is silencing in itself; who wants to get in the way of freedom? The use of the words "free" and "democratic" to describe, and justify, a system which *must* entail some human beings to others is a kind of silencing, Orwellian "newspeak."

If anthropologists take cues from observations made by others across occupations and across regions and nations, what can we learn when we look more closely at the uses of silence and strategic alterity, and what is being obscured by them in a particular thought style? For example, in South Carolina, the confederate flag debate has, in public discourse, been drawn in racialized terms: black and white. But what that masks is the ability to see the struggle in class terms, as well as the ways in which individuals did *not* fall into neatly racialized positions for or against the flag, just as they do not necessarily take positions on anti-immigrant legislation that mirror their racialized identities. Whose voices were completely silenced by seeing all conflicts through the lens of black and white in South Carolina? In the 1989 U.S. Census responses, for example, 67,344 individuals identified themselves as *other* than Black or White. Latinos, Asian Americans, and Native Americans in South Carolina often find that public discourse silences their very presence in the state. If we look at the intersections of age, identity, and income, we can see reasons for struggle in South Carolina that are strategically silenced. According to U.S. Census schedules, in 1989, for example, of individuals 75 and older who lived alone, 36 percent of those who identified as White lived below the poverty level; 46 percent of those who identified as Asian/Pacific Islander lived below the poverty level; 72 percent of those who identified as Black lived below the poverty level; and 82 percent of those who identified as American Indian lived below the poverty level. There is lots to talk about in South Carolina, but discussions of economic inequality and its intersection with a history of racialized oppression and privilege, along various axes of strategic alterity [or through what Patricia Hill Collins (2000) calls the "matrix of domination"], are silenced. Those silences are populated by voices we can professionally attend to as engaged listeners, sharing in a different notion of "free speech."

Something I heard in both the discussion of Proposition 187 and the discussion about the confederate battle flag was the notion that the media covering the different positions were promoting racism or inventing conflict where there was none. This phenomenon of silencing the debate or conflict is akin to what Carol J. Greenhouse (1992: 247) calls "the avoidance ethic" in U.S. society. Robin Sheriff (2000) has theorized this process as "cultural censorship," arguing that anthropologists need to study the various motivations for silencing public discourse. If attending to all positions in the public sphere, and not just the silencing dominant view, is making trouble, then may anthropologists long be troublemakers. Then again, this is not so simple. What is the difference between speaking up as a troublemaker for inclusiveness and one (like Maurice Bessinger) for exclusiveness? It was interesting to see the confederate battle flag come down and the U.S. flag go up, at half mast, in front of Maurice's Barbecue restaurants around South Carolina for two weeks (and only two weeks) following the explosive events of 11 September, 2001. Did Maurice Bessinger see himself, for a moment, as part of a national *communitas* as a new strategic alterity took shape? This one brought with it renewed violence against those not marked as white Native Americans, Asian Americans, Latin Americans, and more (cf. Southern Poverty Law Center 2001 on hate crimes following the events of 9/11/01). What can residents of the U.S. learn from those in other nations about the implications of silence and struggles for symbolic control of freedom of expression," as documented in other chapters of this volume?

Notes

1. For a lengthier, and more ethnographic, discussion of Proposition 187 and strategic alterity, see Kingsolver (2001).
2. The Pioneer Fund has a website which states the aims of the organization and used to have several pages dedicated to rebutting arguments made by journalists and scholars that it has white supremacist goals. In one of those pages (Pioneer Fund), available earlier, representatives of the Pioneer Fund claimed that equating eugenics with genocide is unfair, and the text went on to list prominent U.S. eugenicists including President Theodore Roosevelt and John Harvey Kellogg in a rhetorical move I presume to be akin to invoking character witnesses.
3. Project USA (2002) reported that the organization received a settlement on 23 December, 2002, from the New York/ New Jersey Port Authority after removing one of its anti-immigration billboards.
4. Discussions of free speech in relation to the confederate battle flag have not only focused on the statehouse. In 1991, a South Carolina public school cancelled Black History Month celebrations citing racial tension over the wearing or display of the confederate flag. DePalma (1991: A16) reported a recent purchaser of a confederate flag as saying: "They say this is all about freedom of speech. Well, this [the flag] is speech." K. Michael Prince (2004: 10) says about the confederate flag that it is both a "concrete, history-bound symbol and an unbound, free-floating symbol." Both its meanings and its modes of signification are multiple, and speech seems to be one of those modes that is contested legally. Patricia Williams (1995:128) has noted that there is more tolerance in U.S. public discourse for the confederate flag than for the

swastika as a multivalent symbol ranging from hate speech to nostalgia, and we need to examine why.

5. Prince (2004) notes that confederate symbols have been inserted into public space in South Carolina at strategic moments: the confederate soldiers' monument erected during Reconstruction (Prince 2004: 24); the confederate battle flag being displayed in the South Carolina House of Representatives in 1938 just after the anti-lynching bill supported by the Roosevelt administration was withdrawn from legislative consideration in South Carolina (Prince 2004: 28-30); and the confederate battle flag being raised above the statehouse dome in 1962 in a segregated South Carolina at odds with the Kennedy administration (Prince 2004: 37-40).
6. This silent symbolic parking lot battle is reminiscent of the daily symbolic conflict on the Jefferson Davis Highway running by Maurice Bessinger's Piggie Park Barbecue, between commuters' bumper-adorning fish, fish with crosses, fish evolving legs and sporting Darwin's name, and Christian fish marked "truth" eating the Darwinian amphibians.

References Cited

Almaguer, Tomás. 1994. *Racial Fault Lines: The Historical Origins of White Supremacy in California.* Berkeley: University of California Press.

Alvarez, R. Michael, and Tara L. Butterfield. 2000. "The resurgence of nativism in California? The case of Proposition 187 and illegal immigration." *Social Science Quarterly* 81(1):167-179.

American Civil Liberties Union. Hate speech on campus. http://www.aclu.org/library/pbp16.html.

Balibar, Étienne. 1999. "Class racism." In *Race, Identity, and Citizenship: A Reader.* Rodolfo D. Torres, Louis F. Mirón, and Jonathan Xavier Inda, eds., 322-333. Malden, MA: Blackwell Publishers Inc.

Bessinger, Maurice. Maurice's political views in a nutshell: 21st century declaration of independence renewal. Politics and bbq sauce: A study in cowardice and discrimination. (accessed May 15, 2005).

Bowers, Andy. Aryan nations in Idaho. All Things Considered. August 29, 2000. National Public Radio. .

Collins, Patricia Hill. 2000. *Black Feminist Thought: Knowledge, Consciousness, and the Politics of Empowerment.* Second edition. New York: Routledge.

Crenshaw, Carrie. 1997. "Resisting 'whiteness' rhetorical silence." *Western Journal of Communication* 61(3):253-278.
Delgado, Richard. 1999. "Citizenship." In *Race, Identity, and Citizenship: A Reader.* Rodolfo D. Torres, Louis F. Mirón, and Jonathan Xavier Inda, eds., 247-252. Malden, MA: Blackwell.
DePalma, Anthony. 1991. Free speech and the flag, but this time it's the stars and bars. *The New York Times* 3/13; A16.
Donath, Lori. 2002. "Unraveling the confederate flag: Discourse frameworks as ideological constraints." *Texas Linguistic Forum* 44(2): 252-265.
Farmer, Paul. 1993. *AIDS and Accusation: Haiti and the Geography of Blame.* Berkeley: University of California Press.
Federation for American Immigration Reform. Chronology of terror. (accessed May 15, 2005).
_____. 2004. Press release (July 12). Proposition 200: Cutting through the rhetoric and getting to the facts about the Protect Arizona Now Initiative. (accessed April 21, 2005).
Finnigan, David. 1994. "Hate crimes up since Proposition 187, group says." *National Catholic Reporter* 12/29; 32(10):6(1).
Foucault, Michel. 1979. *Discipline and Punish: The Birth of the Prison.* Translated by Alan Sheridan. New York: Vintage Books.
Frank, Dana. 1999. *Buy American: The Untold Story of Economic Nationalism.* Boston: Beacon Press.
Geertz, Clifford. 1977. *The Interpretation of Cultures.* New York: Basic Books.
Greenhouse, Carol J. 1992. "Signs of quality: Individualism and hierarchy in American culture." *American Ethnologist* 19(2):233-254.
hooks, bell. 2000. *Where We Stand: Class Matters.* New York: Routledge.
Johnson, Kevin R. 1997. "The new nativism: Something old, something new, something borrowed, something blue." In *Immigrants Out!: The New Nativism and the Anti-immigrant Impulse in the United States.* Juan F. Perea, ed. Pp. 165-189. NY: New York University Press.
Kingsolver, Ann E. 2001. *NAFTA Stories: Fears and Hopes in Mexico and the United States.* Boulder, CO: Lynne Rienner Publishers.
Martinez, Demetria. 1995. "Hatred mumbles along new fault lines called Proposition 187." *National Catholic Reporter* 2/10; 31(15):18(1).
Mills, Charles W. 1996. *The Racial Contract.* Ithaca, NY: Cornell University Press.

National Association for the Advancement of Colored People. 2004. Call for action, July 29. NAACP condemns Sudan genocide, reaffirms South Carolina boycott; convention resolutions scheduled for ratification at October meeting. (accessed April 23, 2005).
Omi, Michael, and Howard Winant. 1993. *Racial Formation in the United States from the 1960s to the 1990s.* (Second edition.) New York: Routledge.
Ong, Aihwa. 1999. "Cultural citizenship as subject making: Immigrants negotiate racial and cultural boundaries in the United States." In *Race, Identity, and Citizenship: A Reader.* Rodolfo D. Torres, Louis F. Mirón, and Jonathan Xavier Inda, eds. Pp. 262-293. Malden, MA: Blackwell Publishers Inc.
Ono, Kent A., and John M. Sloop. 2002. *Shifting Borders: Rhetoric, Immigration, and California's Proposition 187.* Philadelphia: Temple University Press.
Ortner, Sherry. 1991. "Reading America: Preliminary notes on class and culture." In *Recapturing Anthropology: Working in the Present.* Richard G. Fox, ed. Pp. 163-189. Santa Fe, NM: School of American Research Press.
_____. 1973. On key symbols. *American Anthropologist* 78:1338-1346.
Papa, Lee, and Luke Eric Lassiter. 2003. "The Muncie race riots of 1967, representing community memory through public performance, and collaborative ethnography between faculty, students, and the local community." *Journal of Contemporary Ethnography* 32(2):147-166.
Pioneer Fund. False charge #10. .
Prince, K. Michael. 2004. *Rally 'Round the Flag, Boys! South Carolina and the Confederate Flag.* Columbia, SC: University of South Carolina Press.
Project USA. Project USA wins free speech settlement in NY lawsuit. Issue 136: December 23, 2002. .
Rodriguez, Gregory. 1997. "The browning of California: Proposition 187 backfires." *The New Republic.* 9/2; 215(10):18(2).
Rosaldo, Renato. 1998. "Cultural citizenship, inequality, and multiculturalism." In *Race, Identity, and Citizenship: A Reader.* Rodolfo D. Torres, Louis F. Mirón, and Jonathan Xavier Inda, eds. Pp. 253-261. Malden, MA: Blackwell Publishers Inc.
Schramm-Pate, Susan L., and Richard Lussier. 2003. "Teaching students how to think critically: The confederate flag controversy in the high school social studies classroom." *High School Journal* 87(2):56-65.

Sheriff, Robin E. 2000. "Exposing silence as cultural censorship: A Brazilian case." *American Anthropologist* 102(1):114-132.
Southern Poverty Law Center. Raging against the other. December 6, 2001.
Staples, Brent. 2002. "South Carolina: The politics of barbecue and the battle of Piggie Park." *The New York Times* 9/16 A1 & A16.
Stefancic, Jean. 1997. "Funding the nativist agenda." In *Immigrants Out!: The New Nativism and the Anti-immigrant Impulse in the United States.* Juan F. Perea, ed. Pp. 119-135. NY: New York University Press.
Taussig, Michael. 1987. *Shamanism, Colonialism, and the Wild Man: A Study in Terror and Healing.* Chicago: The University of Chicago Press.
Turner, V. 1970. *Forest of Symbols: Aspects of Ndembu Ritual.* Ithaca: Cornell University Press.
United Press International. 2000. NAACP continues boycott over Confederate flag. October 16. p1008289u7925.
Williams, Patricia J. 1995. Ignorance and significance. *Index on Censorship* 24(5):126-128.
Zavella, Patricia. 1997. "The tables are turned: Immigration, poverty, and social conflict in California communities." In *Immigrants Out!: The New Nativism and the Anti-immigrant Impulse in the United States.* Juan F. Perea, ed. Pp. 136-161. NY: New York University Press.

Chapter 5

No/Ma(i)ds: Silenced Subjects in Philippine Migration[1]

Pauline Gardiner Barber

> ... identity is always an open, complex, unfinished game—always under construction ... it always moves into the future by means of a symbolic detour through the past... .It produces new subjects who bear the traces of the specific discourses which not only formed them but enable them to produce themselves anew and differently. (Hall 1993: 362)

The Argument

Close to one million people leave the Philippines annually to work abroad. They contribute billions of pesos in remittances. More than 70 percent of these migrants are women who work in service sector jobs located pretty much all over the world with the exception of countries too impoverished to support an influx of foreign workers.[2] Despite continuing public discussion about its relatively rapid growth and increasingly gendered character, first apparent in the 1980s, relatively little ethnographic attention was accorded Philippine migration until recently (Chang and Groves 2000; Constable 1997, 1999; Groves and Chang 1999; Parreñas 2001). Moreover, as I will argue here, there remains a curious silence about the sustained material and class effects of Philippine migration. The economic and social transformations that result from remittances and the normalization of overseas migration are relatively unexplored, hence the Philippines in the literature seems undynamic, an impoverished "developing" nation frozen in time. Further, the contributions to the Philippine econ-

omy from remittances originating in women's labor seem less remarkable in the ethnographic literature than the exploitative dimensions of their contracts. Both of these features of contemporary Philippine experience could and should be more balanced ethnographically.

Paradoxically, I suggest the relative silence about migration's class consequences may have something to do with the gendering of the migration flow which pushes subjective and familial concerns to the foreground, for researchers, for migrants, and in national discussions about Philippine economic reliance upon migration. Also at play, however, are theoretical conventions which obscure or refuse the legitimacy of class concerns and, indeed, class theory (for example, Lem and Leach 2002; Sider 2004; Smith 1999). Class becomes dislodged from any central role in subject formation as other identities and their fluidity are privileged. Finally, I suggest the siting of migration fieldwork, a matter of ethnographic methodology, is also a factor in how class issues are marginalized or located just "off the page" when labor migration is represented ethnographically. Most studies are located outside the Philippines and the stories are told in particular migration sites in scripted ways, typically commencing with narratives of hardship. Here I approach the elision of social class in writing about Philippine labor migration through a number of different ethnographic angles. But first, I review common themes in the main representational conventions.

Despite their differing logic and readers, several discursive conventions characterize both scholarly and popular writing on Philippine women labor migrants. In both sorts of writing, women are cast as victims and/or heroines, and sometimes both. The case is made through reference to historical distortions in Philippine political economy tied in the first instance to the Spanish and American colonial periods and, subsequently, to the legacies of corruption seen most aggressively through the Marcos period of intensive yet uneven modernization. Political economy thus sets the scene for women's victimization and it frames their heroic response as in the commonly heard explanation for why women migrate: "they are helping their families and saving the nation."

In contrast to more structurally determining claims and counter claims, a recent post structural corrective is seen mainly in ethnographic work crediting women's agency by exploring the multiple possibilities of migration experience, its nuance and subjective complexity. Here, Nicole Constable's 1997 ethnography *Maid to Order in Hong Kong: Stories of Filipina Workers* is foundational. Concerned with migrant agency, she examines migration histories through interviews, participation in migration support agencies, and through correspondence in *Tinig Filipino*, a migrant newsletter. The migrant agency she exemplifies does not sustain a viable change-oriented political strategy. Rather she describes agency as self-disciplining subversion of political potential. Foucault more than Marx, or Gramsci guides her reading of resistance. Also in Hong Kong, Groves and Chang (1999) offer a methodologically innovative review of different interpretive possibilities for understanding Philippine migrants' agency and cultural politics. Here again, Philippine gendered cultural politics hold sway as some women counter racialized public challenges to their sexuality by calling for fellow migrants to express an "ethic of service." Both projects suggest what I call a Janus (double-faced) quality of migrant agency (Barber 2002, 2004). They show how migrants' actions to assert control and dignity rebound against them. But I offer an alternative reading. These examples, I suggest, reveal powerlessness AND empowerment.

There are, then, two aligned yet potentially contradictory themes in the discourse; Philippine women as victims, and/or heroines constituted historically through circumstances which arise from colonial political economy and globalization. Yet migrants are also women who engage in migration scenarios as agents. A central concern of this chapter is to contrast these dichotomous themes, not so much to overturn them, for each relies on histories and positionalities that condition and comprise migration experience. Rather, it will be proposed here that Philippine migration can be understood through a dialectical rendering of materiality and subjectivity, not as discursive oppositions but of a piece.

Detailed readings of migration narratives thus confirm contested negotiation between structure and agency. Most important to my purpose here, they also expose classed subjectivities as a critical aspect of migration. This is the most curious form of silencing given that labor migration is mainly about class as lived experience, as identity, and as contestation within the labor contract. Migration narratives in popular press and in ethnographic interviews are here seen as confirming the exploitative aspects of labor migration along somewhat predictable lines as sketched above. However, they can also be read as histories of struggle, surely a classed experience. Moreover, class effects are apparent in Philippine migrant sending communities which remain unexplored by ethnographic inquiry conducted in migrant receiving contexts, the siting of the new post-structural ethnography sketched above.

In what follows, I explore migration as process and practice through various ethnographic encounters. These provide further evidence of how material and subjective renderings of migration can be silenced through

discursive conventions and theoretical orientations. The predominant silence in Philippine labor migration is revealed, in concluding, to be that of its classed effects.

Mapping the Locality

Let me set the scene by briefly describing how migration is woven into the fabric of Philippine life and livelihood, ever present yet sometimes overlooked. The ethnographic context is two communities in the Visayan region of the Philippines. My first encounter with Philippine out-migration was by chance.[3] In the early 1990s I was visiting some coastal communities with a group of Philippine environmental researchers concerned about coastal resource degradation in Bais Bay, approximately one hour's bus ride from Dumaguete city on the island of Negros. While most of the attention of the group was directed to the physical environment, our discussion turned to questions of culture and community in "participatory appraisal" discussions with invited community representatives. At these meetings we learned much about the livelihood struggles of local people whom my colleagues readily classified as "fisherfolk." Because of my longstanding interest in livelihood complexity in Canadian working-class households and for reasons having to do with serendipity in the seating arrangements for the meeting, I became curious about some modest yet observable differences in household "wealth." Discussions at the meeting focused on fishers' routines and needs. Alternative or complementary livelihood practices were not much explored. Locals at the meeting knew we were there to discuss fisheries so they concentrated upon fishing related issues plus other predictable difficulties of daily life. Mostly, they described problems stemming from unreliable cash income and their limited access to resources of all kinds. Life and livelihood came across as a daily survival struggle with few contingencies outside of social resources and the social capital they provide. We also learned about inadequate services, most memorably potable water during the driest months but all services were tenuous and in need of upgrading.

Back at the university our discussions all too quickly linked poverty to environmental degradation and livelihood security to environmental sustainability. Extra community processes in political economy (for example Philippine indebtedness and regional economic disparities, the bedrock of regional labor migration) seemed beyond the scope of the task at hand. Subsequently the environmental sustainability concerns were translated into a series of linked "community-based resource management" programs of action, mostly directed towards correcting resource degradation in the marine and upland environments. Several modest initiatives targeted livelihood diversification premised in part on the logic that such diversification might relieve livelihood pressures.

With no pretension of expertise in resource management planning and in keeping with my observer/outsider status, I was intrigued by a chance encounter that happened as I wandered around the meeting site, my attention drifting from plans to draw inventories of fish stock and sea grasses. I was an incongruous figure in that time and place. Daisy spotted me through her window and quickly emerged, her curiosity getting the better of her morning's planned trip to the market. She responded to my story about our investigation of local livelihood problems with her complicated story of sequential migration experiences. She had recently returned from her third overseas labor contract in Hong Kong and was brooding over the arrival of news about a further contract. Her house seemed modest, even by local standards, which did not fit the pattern I later learned to read of housing upgrades as possible symbolic evidence of migration "success." She told me she lived with her son, then a young adult, a college graduate who would soon embark on his own labor migration seeking work beyond the deskilling environs of local labor markets. Employment for young men was scarce but in the immediate area there was occasional day labor on small haciendas, in municipal work crews, and sometimes as crew in modest fishing enterprises such as handheld net fishing. All such employment was sporadic at best and opportunities were distributed through complex social arrangements. Sequential development projects also provided periodic employment options for guards, drivers, and technicians, but such prospects were unlikely for commerce graduates such as Daisy's son, or for people like herself who apparently lacked locally productive patronage networks.

While Daisy was scornful about the prospects for community economic development, she was less cynical about her own future. Despite her modest dwelling, she was relatively well-off, she said. Her wealth was in her livestock, cows and pigs farmed through contractual arrangements with neighbors. A subsequent conversation with one of Daisy's neighbors, one of the few women present in the meeting rather than on the periphery, provided further clue when she spoke of her neighbor's husband's drinking. The neighbor was Daisy, the husband a drain on her resources and perhaps explanation for her cynicism.

I was curious about Daisy's explanation of the discrepancy between her seemingly modest living circumstances and the more cosmopolitan flair she brought to our conversation. And so began my further investigation of spatially displaced migrant livelihood in "fishing households" in this, the poorest of several coastal *barangays* in Bais.[4] Daisy returned to Hong Kong again, maintaining an invisible presence through her modest farming enterprise and continuing her claim to property. In several trips to Bais in the intervening years, I noticed her house was increasingly dwarfed by improvements to surrounding homes. Likely she maintains savings in Hong Kong for her own future, perhaps free from the claims of those who have not played their part in conserving her livelihood contributions, nor been considerate of her effort.

This encounter shows how migration can be silenced discursively through prioritizing strategies in development discourse—in this case environmental sciences took precedence. Also, pragmatic livelihood diversity was reductively narrowed into a singular occupation through the functional nomination of fishing as primary. More than this, a subtle yet long-standing gender discrimination was at play in attributing primary livelihood significance to the activities of men—"men fish here, women glean and sell fish." As subsequent research on gendered livelihoods in Bais clarified (Barber 1995, 1996), women's labor is more diverse and comprises the greater component of livelihood in this, and apparently many other, Philippine communities (Illo and Polo 1990; Tacoli 1995). Such gendered forms of silence seem "old hat" by now but they bear repeating here because they provide foundational direction to the complexities of structure and agency in Philippine migration. Just as the primary economic actors in coastal areas are presumed to be masculine, the livelihood slots accorded migration's victims and heroines are feminized, as is the migration flow. Could it also be that in attending to gendered effects of Philippine migration, the class effects remain silenced precisely because the migration is feminized? Certainly this fits a long-standing struggle in feminist scholarship to have women's productive efforts and consequence duly acknowledged, theoretically and practically.

I suggest we need to return to these issues to avoid an even more profound form of discursive silencing stemming from a narrowly theorized post-structuralism where narrativizing focuses upon the victimized rather than the agentic voice, the disempowered rather than the potentially empowered. Narrative accounts of migration experience highlight the drama of migration in a manner that reveals cultural complicity rather than the class effects of migration. In part this stems from a gendering of migration experience where women's livelihood through migration becomes less significant than the fact that they are women migrants separated from home, family, and nation. Such concerns condition Philippine gendered migration narratives and play into its victimizing/heroic dichotomies in discourse.

Migration and Materiality

From a Philippine local perspective migration resonates in daily life. For well over twenty years remittances contributed support to various households in Bais coastal *barangays.* As a matter of routine Bais residents have long traveled to other Philippine labor markets, mainly Manila, and overseas, mainly to Southeast Asia. Several women have migrated to Canada and were introduced to me by their neighbors in Bais as fellow Canadian citizens. In terms of material conditions, labor migration has underscored three main types of economic changes. In housing construction, native wooden building materials have been replaced with concrete structures. In educational support, money has assisted in extending the education of daughters, sons, nieces, and nephews. And, to a lesser extent, remittances have contributed capital for the purchase, repair, and updating of fishing gear (for example, small boats or *banca* and weirs and nets), also for small businesses (a motorized tricycle for a taxi service and start-up funds for several small convenience *sari sari* stores). Remittances also contribute to increased consumption mainly seen in the acquisition of appliances such as television sets. They also purchase health care services and medicine. This inventory of the material consequences of migration in Bais communities became the basis for my comparison of the effects of migration in another Philippine context.

The second field site commenced from research in Iloilo city in Panay. The social networks through which I came to understand Iloilo's patterns of migration soon extended from the city proper to the periphery, where livelihood practices include agriculture, primarily rice farming, market gardening, and livestock production. These networks were initially constructed through my university-based activities and my colleagues' introductions to their friends, students, and neighbors. In this more spatially dispersed site remittance spending is similar to Bais. Indeed, over the ten years since Daisy guided my initial immersion into its complexities, women's labor migration has continued to increase in scale and be accommodated to in quotidian life in Philippine communities.

Educational aspirations often incorporate the possibility of overseas migration, and the education of women for skilled service sector jobs has increased commensurate with particular migration flows. For example, a fluctuating demand in overseas labor markets for nurses and caregivers encourages nursing and midwifery education, the latter being less costly. It is not surprising then that in Iloilo communities the education of younger siblings and their children, as well as one's own children, emerges as a major motivation for migration. It is one of the most common initial targets of cash remittances. Housing upgrades also figure significantly in migrants' plans. Typically the women's parents' house is the first priority, followed by the women's own nuclear household. Sometimes, women continue to live with their parents or they may build a small structure on land adjacent to their parents' property. Some unmarried women imagine their working lives in a prolonged series of migration contracts—although there are few guarantees. In such cases funds are primarily directed toward meeting the needs of others since personal savings are hard to justify when the needs of one's relatives are pressing. But all migrants are called upon to provide assistance to kin with requests flowing through the carefully cultivated social capital networks that both constitute and are constituted as Philippine livelihood.

In the more urbanized context of Iloilo where I now concentrate my research efforts, I have become familiar with a much larger pool of migrant households. Iloilo women confirm that they also experience conflicting financial pressures during their overseas work contracts and have difficulty saving money given the many claims on their modest earnings. Migrants' housing projects are at various stages of completion and because of the insecurities of local labor markets, some have already set up small-small enterprises which they hope to expand with savings from planned future migrations. Others have contributed money to family projects, one example being the purchase of a husband's *tricycle*, a taxi service for local passengers. Further initiatives include development of a "warehouse" for storing rice surpluses purchased in the harvest season for later sale at an increased price, surely a class practice in the Marxian sense. Carmen's business prepares food for sale to commuters on a busy highway, while her cousin plans to start a "*buy and sell*" business in quality used clothing. Most likely because of the greater range of possibilities offered by population density, and the more complexly classed nature of Iloilo migration, future plans typically include some form of business project beyond agriculture, more so than in Bais. But some women with kin in rural areas have set their hopes on purchasing more land for rice farming, or increasing the size of livestock holdings, such as pigs. Again, access to and control over resources define the imperatives underlying migration. This makes it all the more remarkable that the migration literature accords more attention to the sacrificial victimized subjectivity than the class empowered one. My point is that these are not mutually exclusive positions.

On the other hand, it must also be said that many women who have completed multiple overseas contracts continue to seek further work because they have been unable to realize any personal savings. When they report "this time I will try harder to save," they also fear the various claims upon their wages will continue to jeopardize future plans. Here is the flip side of the Janus face of migration: the risk of thwarted material promise. Increased levels of consumption in Philippine society guarantee constant pressure on women to share their income and savings. Gendered cultural politics which model feminine familial generosity can intensify both pressure and guilt. These feelings must be negotiated if obligations real (in the case of indebtedness) and perceived (in the case of familial generosity) are not acted upon. Even so, most migrants leave the Philippines with resolve to be fiscally prudent. Many financial plans get at least partially executed and there is clear evidence of the role of remittances in the varied local economies represented throughout the Philippines.

While increased consumption seems modest at the individual household level, it is quite dramatic in urban centers. Both Dumaguete and Iloilo have new modern shopping centers with chain stores selling brand name products, designer clothing, and "big ticket" items. They provide clear evidence of the development of Philippine capitalism and new class subjectivities arising from increased gendered migration flows. They also symbolize the routinization of migration in state policy and daily life. In Dumaguete I participated in this class and consumption shift when I hosted the visit to the city of my Bais research assistant and her three young daughters in 1994. We visited a newly opened three-story department store to purchase school supplies and delighted in traveling on the city's first escalator. Aside from purchasing a "fast food" lunch, my contribution to the day's adventure was to pay for the girls' least needed but most highly desired item: three bright pink backpacks adorned with Disney-type cartoon characters. With this purchase their school environment moved one small step closer to a North American school consumption pattern. Other aspects of their schooling and meagre educational resources do not compare; teachers struggle with large class sizes and a lack of basic teaching supplies. How ironic that their pupils now have new consumption standards through which to imagine school attendance. The burden of educational expenses thus increases.

Iloilo is a larger city with a more active migrant sending sector. Most people familiar with the city would likely agree with my university friends that the strongest symbol of the city's migrant strengthened economic base is the newly opened "SM Mega Mall." SM stands for Shoe Mart, a Philippine department store of which there are now two in Iloilo City. Visits with friends to the second SM, the Mega Mall, accompanied by relatives on paid vacation from their Hong Kong employment, revealed ethnographically the links between everyday Philippine microeconomics and the circuits of international capital that migrant labor contributes to. One thing I learned was that the Esprit clothing in the Philippines is sold at a retail cost comparable to its pricing in equivalent Canadian malls. This clothing is expensive from the perspective of Canadian middle-class shoppers—dramatically more so for Philippine consumers. Yet the store has many customers, as do those which sell "knockoff" styles fashioned after Esprit and similar firms.

Migration in Narrative

In the remainder of the chapter, I reference migration experiences collected from migrants who were living in the Philippines when I met them, having completed one or more overseas contracts. Some were contemplating further contracts in Southeast Asian countries. Several had completed more permanent forms of im/migration (for example in Canada, the United States, and Italy) when I met them during one of their periodic return visits to the Philippines. Typically, though not exclusively, the narrative accounts of migration experience the women present to me mirror the stories of hardship reported in the popular press. Mostly, women dwell upon the interlocking themes of hardship (the long tedious hours of work), endurance ("you get used to it"), and the small daily victories (gaining the support of the male boss when the "lady boss" is cruel). Positive aspects of migration tend not to be initially included in the descriptions of migrants' daily routines offered in interviews and in less formal everyday conversation. Rather, positive reflections about migration and its effects upon their lives tend to be situated in the Philippines, spatially and temporally displaced from the migrants' labor process and its social context. Here we see the importance of thinking about the local and global interface and the need for multisited research. In their first response to the question "What was good about migration, for you?" most women follow the predictable gendered cultural logic to speak about their provision of help for family members in the Philippines (the building of houses, the education of younger relatives). At first glance, these are seemingly self-sublimating, rather than empowering projections. I qualify this point because dis/empowerment is not as straightforward as some authors suggest. It has both a cultural and a structural framing that I will explore further below.

On one visit to Iloilo (in August 2000) I concluded my interview conversations with approximately ten women migrants with a more directed discussion of how migration had affected them personally. After recounting the more obvious migration logic of familial economic need, and their different but similar struggles with confining overly harsh employers—plus, in one memorable case, a near rape—several women explicitly spoke of their work as empowering. Herein lies a major challenge for writing the subjects of Philippine labor migration into contemporary migration literature, the subjectivities and material consequences; how to write about and respond to Philippine migration as exploitation and empowerment (as action and reaction). As contradiction? As counterpoint? What are the framing discourses and their implications? What is rendered visible in the quotidian struggles that comprise migration experience and what is obscured from view?

What follows is not the refined synthetic account of my resolution of this problematic. Rather it is a reflection on the ways in which writing about Philippine migration can explicitly and obliquely silence. The complex subjective possibilities in migrants' discursive framing of empowerment need to be balanced against consideration of class and cultural politics, their temporal, social, and spatial complication. The main forms of silencing discussed here—en-route to my major concern about class—reside in popular discourses, emanating from both the state and its critics. Related to this are the sometimes inadvertent, sometimes avoidable theoretical and methodological "silences." It is the matter of class, however, that poses the biggest and most puzzling challenge.

Irrespective of their social origins, Philippine women labor migrants, be they in North America, Europe, or Southeast Asia, have their identities subsumed by names such as Filipina, Nannies, Care-givers (in Canada), Overseas Contract Workers ("OCWs") and Domestic Helpers ("DHs") in the Philippines, and more generically Maids. These labels are inflected and accented with cultural and economic signifiers which presume the buying and selling of women's labor (in demeaned social reproduction employment) to comprise the most important marker of identity. Arguably, "work" is fundamental, although not exclusively so, in the formation of social identities, especially when class practices surrounding the labor process and its social consequences are explored. Paradoxically, however, the gendered connotations of migration nomenclature divert discussion of Philippine migrants as classed subjects. Instead women who migrate are typically construed as victims, either explicitly in the case of calls for policy reform and in sociological accounts of their demeaned domestic work contexts, or implicitly in work that ethnographically "refuses" their forms of resistance (Ortner 1995) in particular contexts. For example, in research that shows how Philippine migrants are constituted as the racialized "other" prone to crime and prostitution in Hong Kong (Groves and Chang 1999), Singapore (Yeoh, Huang, et al. 1999), and Malaysia (Chin 1997), the respective ethnographers present a partial rendering of migrant experience which is compelling and insightful yet still falls back on migrant identity as victimized economic subjects. This identity stands in for a classed subject positioning which, to be well described, likely requires more reference to Philippine realities than is possible from the regional labor markets where the research occurs.[5]

To a lesser extent migrants are also accorded heroine status but here again this reading references a hardworking sacrificial economic subject. Such a subject remains on those rare occasions when migrants are rendered as both victim and heroine, as in the case of Sara Balabagan, the sixteen-year-old woman who was tried for murder in September 1995 in the United Arab Emirates. She was found guilty of stabbing her male employer, whom she claimed had attempted to rape her soon after she arrived. In response to Philippine domestic protests and with widespread international support, the Philippine state managed to have her death sentence reduced to public flogging plus one year in jail. Earlier that same year, in Singapore, Flor Contemplaçion had been tried for murder, ostensibly the outcome of a quarrel between friends (Hilsdon 2000). She was executed despite much public agitation in the Philippines.

Since 1995, which some Philippine observers suggest was the proverbial last straw for Philippine state laissez-faire regarding migrant abuse (Gonzalez 1998), official Philippine reactions to migrant misfortune have become more assertive and proactive. The hastily drawn 1995 Act spells stricter controls over all stages of the migration process. There is also provision made for repatriation and re-entry to Philippine society. The Act signals a deepening commitment to the regulation and routines of an enduring labor migration. Since 1995, Philippine overseas workers are also more often constituted as "hero/ines". For example, the year 2000 was officially dedicated the "year of OFWs" (overseas foreign workers) by

President Estrada. Sara Balabagan returned home to a heroine's welcome in 1996 and has become associated with celebrity, even in Canada. While Balabagan and Contemplaçion are emblematic of the darker, "victimized" side of migration, Sara Balabagan might equally serve as an example of personal empowerment, that is over time and through the shifting sites of her subsequent experience. In May 1999, a Canadian newspaper reported that she had embarked on a singing career. The headline was "Killer Maid Turns to Song." In the Philippines she is defined more sympathetically and is the subject of a widely screened film, the release date for which was stalled while Philippine state officials sought to appease UAE attempts at censorship.

Even with the temporally imposed ambiguities, these examples reveal the silencing of migration through the selective and at times reductive rendering of the multiple meanings and significance of migration into a polarized model. This applies to both discussions of migrant experience and state practices. For example, the accounts of migration and individual labor migrants in Philippine media and popular culture which I have skimmed here represent migration as perilous even as they reinforce and normalize its ordinariness in Philippine society. Such discourses may originate in state affirming valorization of migrant sacrifice wherein migrants are presented as heroic contributors to national development, as they have been since the Marcos administration oversaw the rapid acceleration of Philippine labor migration during the 1980s. But they also surface in the counternarratives of political groups concerned about the state's abnegation of responsibility for its reliance upon migration as the cornerstone of development and its failure to stem migration flows, or to develop more viable economic and social policies.

It is hoped that I have convinced readers about the first part of my argument that various discourses of Philippine women's migration can be read (analyzed) for silences/silencing; in state practices, through the transnational regulation of migration, and in popular media. Silences are also evident in the configuring of scholarly accounts of Philippine migration. Inasmuch as these are confined to one location and political moment, however useful, they remain a situationally bound rendering of migrant identity. Narrowly confined academic research methodologies and theoretical framing may also serve to silence in matters of class and of the instrumentalities of agency. In addition, because the classed aspects of Philippine cultural politics are fraught with ambiguities, they are scarcely discernible in life history narratives collected from a single location. When migrations are tracked through several locations and over time, more socially and temporally dynamic articulations of agency are revealed. Multisited research challenges reductions in various official discourses and reveals their relations of power.

Identity Detours

I am arguing that discourses of Philippine labor migration (popular and academic) simplify the complexities of migrant identity in ways which elide the contingencies of power in the various geographically, socially, and culturally dispersed sites where migrants live, travel to and work. Moreover, if, as Stuart Hall (1993) reminds us identity also entails a symbolic revisiting and reworking of the past, then the various discourses surrounding Philippine women's migration are also prone to mis/take the present and the future. This occurs because migration is read off from a temporal present to produce a linear and selective representation of migration, both personal and national. This is a rather abstracted way of suggesting that when migrant experiences are represented, their viewpoints reflect some but not all aspects of their experiences and what is often recounted obscures rather than reveals the more everyday struggles over identity, power, and class positioning that characterize migration, now normalized in everyday experience. Different articulations of the meaning of migration are possible at different moments, in different sites, and for different audiences. Moreover, as suggested earlier, the continuous reading of migration as a narrative of hardship for migrants and the nation renders the Philippine economy as frozen in time, located outside of globalization orbits and dialogues about alternative modernities.

This brings me to the proposition that the class problematic—how to read class and its interpellation with cultural practices, and how these might flow from and to Philippine political scenarios—is perhaps the most striking, indeed powerful silence in writing about Philippine migration. This is surely paradoxical. Overall, my research in Philippine communities and with Philippine migrants resident in Canada suggests class shifts are occurring in Philippine communities and in the lives of migrants who assume a longer-term diasporic positioning. This is certainly true for women migrants who entered Canada under the domestic caregivers program, a visa condition that allows applicants to apply for permanent residency and landed immigrant status if certain conditions are met. For all the critical attention this program has rightfully received (Bakan and Stasiulis 1997), it also needs to be said that Canadian destinations and their difficulties are judged differently from locations in Philippine communities.

But more generally also, women's migrant labor produces shifts in class, consumption and social patterns in Philippine communities. I hasten to add that some changes are minor and many are contradictory for the new cultural practices and subject (class) positioning they give rise to. However, such an outcome is surely, at the very least, partly the point of so-called development; that is, of the marking out of Philippine women's differentness (Hall 1993), their positioning in transnational development policies, their disadvantageous labor contracts; all of which contribute to draw ever widening groups of Filipinos into new circuits of production and consumption, albeit in terribly exploited ways (Harvey 2000).

The fact that large numbers of Philippine women commit themselves to migration—many now plan their lives around it—and the circuits of exchange set in motion through their struggles translate into class shifts in Philippine communities. This needs more explicit theoretical and ethnographic attention. And, as feminist scholars propose, this attention should take account of women's "standpoints" which, at the risk of repeating myself, I am proposing cannot be read off from either the political or the culturally pronounced discourses of Philippine women's (catholicized) appeals to national and familial duty. Class theorists such as Harvey (1995, 2000), Sider (2004), Smith (1999), and, importantly for many anthropologists, Raymond Williams (1989) remind us that dignity remains one of the most powerful components of classed subjectivity. For migrants, there is a dignity in "duty" if not labor, however fraught this may be. Some women reference their migration as an escape from marital distress, or their sexual subordination, others see migration as an exile they willfully engage (Tacoli 1999).

Countering this, it also needs to be said that many women end up in repeat cycles of migration because the grim economic realities they contend with cannot be "worked off" through one migration cycle—typically two years in Southeast Asian regional labor markets. Some migrants take on sequential labor contracts because the layers of exploitation they are exposed to commence with their own domestic environs, from within their households, from husbands and kin who garner interest on loans and/or compete to consume the meagre earnings remitted home.

My research suggests that for most migrants, however, migration is always about more than these brute facts. Moreover, class shifts are not necessarily only important in-as-much as they might become collectively-politically-socially transformative, as some migration critics would have it. Some aspects of migration are recorded positively by women migrants and a continuing desire for class-based mobility is the bedrock of the current scale of women's labor migration. As noted earlier, most migrants imagine themselves or family members as becoming small-scale entrepreneurs as a result of the migration process. Related to this, they want to increase their capacities to consume various consumer goods that mark Philippine households as middle-class. The ethnographic evidence of these changes is apparent throughout the Philippines, perhaps most obviously visually apparent in newly constructed concrete houses on family properties or in housing estates, and as noted, in new commercial developments. Migrants also particularly want to increase the levels of education acquired by family members, and sometimes themselves. There is more than economic disempowerment at play here, as is nicely captured in the ethnographic work which re-presents the "cultural surface" of migrant discourses of migrant sacrifice, suffering, and romanticized notions of community. To read these discourses at face value, this new work implicitly suggests, is to reproduce the idea that Philippine migrants are structurally disempowered victims; a conclusion some writers return to despite the variability of experiences they record (for example, Constable 1997). Other recent studies besides my own (for example, Chang and Groves 2000; Constable 1999) reveal migrant experience to be more diverse, ambivalent, contradictory, and often hopeful than is predicted in many earlier accounts. Nonetheless, the discourses of suffering and tragedy are often called upon to highlight the structural inequities that underlie Philippine migration generally. To me, this juxtaposition of migrant agency and structural constraint produces an unresolved tension, which enables the historically victimizing accounts to hold sway. The cultural and positional politics associated with attributing agency and empowerment in migration scenarios are especially challenging and push beyond simple binary explanations about individual and collective politics and the matter of social transformation. Ironically, the historically victimizing accounts may be all about class but they also deny its re/workings through gendered labor migration.

Thus the silences in the superficially competing discourses (migrants as victims, migrants as heroines) suggest a rewriting, or more correctly, the repositioning of structure with agency in migration literature. These concepts appear to have lost their theoretical efficacy in the preoccupations of post-structural writing. Structure and agency's dialectic commences from but moves beyond the structural legacies of Philippine colonial history. This legacy provides the framework for migration. It conditions migration but it does not contain, circumscribe, nor predetermine migrant experience. Put differently, Philippine structural disempowerment with its obvious class disparities and social consequences should not distract our attention from migrant agency and class dynamics. Nor should it encourage a reading of Philippine history that reproduces historical victims translated into the present, either in Philippine locales or their diaspora spaces (Brah 1996). As Hall (1993) and before him Eric Wolf (1982) affirm, Philippine women migrants, new laborers that they are in regional and far-flung labor markets, are reworking their identities, their gendered understandings of class and cultural practices in Philippine culture and how to "translate" these in their new social sites. In writing (here and elsewhere) on Philippine migration, the power in its silences, I hope to show how Philippine women can be more ethnographically present/ed, their class aspirations more considered and their imagined communities less taken-for-granted.

Listen to these contributors to Tinig Filipina (cited in Chang and Groves 2000), a newsletter produced by Hong Kong based Philippine migrant workers as they translate state narratives and counternarratives into their own common-sense-making of migration experience.

> Through your good works in those places where you are temporarily working, you will become instruments in the economic improvement or progress of your "sick nation" through the dollars you send back home. In the future, through your perseverance and hard work, your children and your children's children will be the ones to benefit from your nation's progress. (Layosa 1994: 6)

and,

> With this very inspiring title "hero," I could walk straight with my head up high in the busy streets of the hot city of Manila. It is indeed very flattering. Whew! I'm a hero. In my little peaceful town of Sanchez Mia, I'm improving my life and most of all, I'm a dollar earner—much more than other people in higher ranks. (Estabillo 1994: 10)

Are we to read positive reflections such as these as variants on a theme of false consciousness, as grist for the mill of structural subjugation? Certainly, the referencing of an imagined future national benefit arising out of the present hardships tempts critical deflation. However, what I emphasize is an alternative Janus-like reading of the complexities of power in migration narratives.

For the last word on migration's social complexity and its traveling class relations, here is what Maribel told me:

> We go there (Hong Kong) as a domestic helper and they look at us as a slave, a maid or a slave. And, when we work there, some of the Filipina, we say that if our employer is so very abusive or arrogant, we can say to ourselves that although we work for them, we are only making money. In our place we are not like this.

I ask her to compare working life in Hong Kong and the Philippines. Class remains her theme.

> In freedom, at least, I prefer here. When you work here it's okay. When you don't have work, you can eat. There it's different. If people do not work, they cannot eat because they cannot pay the rent. So they get maids so that they can work. If they will not get a maid then they will not work. Not all Chinese who get a maid are rich. Some hire maids because they need to work also, to earn more. So even though we have less money here, we can live better.

She concluded our discussion with a description of the material things she hoped to realize through one or two subsequent labor contracts in Southeast Asia.

Notes

1. The Social Sciences and Humanities Research Council (SSHRC) provided funding for a substantial component of this research from 1999 to 2002. Two smaller research fellowships (1992-1994) were also awarded through Canadian International Development (CIDA) funded projects, university partnerships linking Dalhousie University and several institutions in the Philippines for curriculum development and resource management initiatives. Many people in the Philippines, Canada, and Hong Kong have contributed to this research for which I remain enormously grateful. However, I must particularly credit Ginggay, Meloy, and Rose whose introductions proved invaluable. Migration researchers Dr. Stella Go and Dr. Maruja Asis in Manila are also extraordinarily generous colleagues who have always made me feel welcome in my all-too-brief visits to their institutions.
2. In 1998 foreign exchange remittances amounted to US $4,925.31. In that year, official records show 755,684 deployed overseas workers (Philippine Overseas Employment Administration 1999). Unpublished POEA statistics for 2000 show an increase to 841,628 workers deployed. Interestingly, the published figures are not broken down by gender, but I was told that women now comprise close to 70 percent of overseas workers. In some countries such as Hong Kong, the migration flow is mostly female; for example in 1995, 92.8 percent of migrants deployed were women

(Go 1998). Of course, these figures describe workers who travel with official documents. There are many workers who leave the Philippines without encountering POEA document processing routines. For example, some recruiters locate contract workers who agree to travel on tourist visas despite POEA monitoring. Also, the 1995 Migrant Workers and Overseas Filipinos Act includes various incentives and protections to discourage undocumented migration. Some Filipinos continue to risk this "outlaw" travel (Bauman 1998) out of desperation. Others seek to save on costs through drawing on their social networks. Either way, the scale of undocumented migration is hard to predict but likely continues to be considerable.

3. An extended discussion of this example also appears in my essay "Ethnography's Edge in Development" in Meneley and Young, 2005.
4. A *barangay* is the smallest political unit in the Philippines. The three coastal *barangays* from which participation at the meeting was drawn comprised approximately 1,600 households in 1990.
5. In saying this, I appreciate the initiative of these studies for I have learned much from them—indeed, Constable (1999) recognizes that she has understated the importance of class matters in her earlier research.

References Cited

Bakan, Abigail and Davia Stasiulis. 1997. *Not One of the Family: Foreign Domestic Workers in Canada.* Toronto: University of Toronto Press.

Barber, Pauline Gardiner. 1995. "Invisible labor, transnational Lives: Gendered work and new social fields in coastal Philippines." *Culture,* 15(2): 3-26.

_____ 1996. "Modes of resistance: Gendered responses to global impositions in coastal Philippines." *Asia Pacific Viewpoint,* 37(2): 3-26.

_____ 2002. "Envisaging power in Philippine migration: The janus effect." In *Rethinking Empowerment.* J. Parpart, K. Staudt, and G. Youngs eds. London: Routlege.

_____ 2004. "Contradictions of class and consumption when the commodity is labor." *Anthropologica,* 46(2): 203-218.

Bauman, Zygmunt. 1998. *Globalization: The Human Consequences.* New York: Columbia University.

Brah, Avtar. 1996. *Cartograhies of Diaspora: Contesting Identities.* London: Routledge.

Chang, Kimberly and Julian McAllister Groves. 2000. "Neither "saints" nor "prostitutes": Sexual discourse in the Filipina domestic worker community in Hong Kong." *Women's Studies International Forum,* 23(1) 73-87.

Chin, Christine B. 1997. "Walls of silence and late twentieth century representations of the foreign female domestic worker: The case of Filipina and Indonesian female servants in Malaysia." *The International Migration Review*, 31(2): 353-385.

Constable, Nicole. 1997. *Maid to order in Hong Kong: Stories of Filipina workers.* Ithaca: Cornell University Press.

_____ 1999. "At home but not at home: Filipina narratives of ambivalent returns." *Cultural Anthropology,* 14(2): 203-228.

Estabillo, Gloria. 1994. "Into Thy Hands." Tinig Filipino. April: 6.

Go, Stella. 1998. "Towards the 21st Century: Whither Philippine Labor Migration?" In *Filipino Workers on the Move: Trends, Dilemmas and Policy Options.* Benjamin Cariño ed. Manila: Philippine Migration Research Network, Philippine Social Science Council.

Gonzalez, Joaquin L. III. 1998. *Philippine Labor Migration: Critical Dimensions of Public Policy.* Singapore: Institute of Southeast Asian Studies and De La Salle University Press

Groves, Julian McAllister and Kimberly Chang. 1999. "Romancing resistance and resisting romance." *Journal of Contemporary Ethnography,* 28(3): 554-557.

Hall, Stuart. 1993. " Culture, Community, Nation." *Cultural Studies,* 4(3): 349-363.

Harvey, David. 1995. "Militant particularism and global Ambition: The conceptual politics of place, space and environment in the work of Raymond Williams." *Social Text,* 42 (Spring): 69-98.

_____ 2000. *Spaces of Hope.* Berkeley: University of California Press.

Hilsdon, Anne-Marie. 2000. "The Contemplaçion fiasco: The hanging of a Filipino domestic worker in Singapore." In *Human Rights and Gender Politics: Asia-Pacific Perspectives.* Anne-Marie Hilsdon, Martha Macintyre, Vera Mackie and Maila Stivens (eds). London: Routledge pp172-92.

Illo, Jeanne and Jaime Polo. 1990. *Fishers, Traders, Farmers, Wives: The Life Stories of Ten Women in a Fishing Village.* Manila: Institute of Philippine Culture, Ateneo de Manila University.

Layosa, Linda. 1994. "Where Do I Stand?" Tinig Filipino. March: 10.

Lem, Winnie and Belinda Leach, eds. 2002. *Culture, Economy, Power: Anthropology as Critique, Anthropology as Praxis.* Albany: State University of New York Press.
Meneley, Anne and Donna Young (eds). 2005. *Auto-ethnographies of Academic Practice.* Peterborough: Broadview Press.
Ortner, Sherry. 1995. "Resistance and the problem of ethnographic refusal." *Comparative Studies in Society and History,* 34(1): 173-93.
Parreñas, Rachel Salazar. 2001. *Servants of Globalization: Women, Migration and Domestic Work. Stanford*: Stanford University Press.
Philippine Overseas Employment Administration. 1999. *Overseas Employment Statistics* 1982-1998. Manila: Philippine Overseas Employment Administration, Planning Branch.
Sider, Gerald. 2004. *Between History and Tomorrow: Making and Breaking Everyday Life in Newfoundland.* Peterborough: Broadview Press.
Smith, Gavin. 1999. *Contronting the Present: Towards a Politically Engaged Anthropology.* Oxford: Berg Publishing.
Tacoli, Cecilia. 1995. "Gender and international survival strategies: A research agenda with reference to Filipina labor migrants in Italy." *Third World Planning Review,* 17(2): 199-212.
_____ 1999. "International migration and the restructuring of gender asymmetries: Continuity and change among Filipino labor migrants in Rome." *The International Migration Review,* 33(3): 658-682.
Yeoh, Brenda, Shirlena Huang, et al. 1999. 'Migrant female domestic workers: Debating the economic, social and political impacts in Singapore.' *The International Migration Review,* 33(1): 114-136.
Williams, Raymond. 1989. *Resources of Hope.* London: Verso.
Wolf, Eric R. 1982. *Europe and the People Without History.* Berkeley: University of California Press.

Chapter 6

The Muzzled Saint: Racism, Cultural Censorship, and Religion in Urban Brazil

Robin E. Sheriff

After visiting Brazil in 1940-1941, the African-American sociologist, E. Franklin Frazier remarked, "There is in Brazil, little discussion of the racial or color situation. It appears that there is an unexpressed understanding among all elements of the population not to discuss the racial situation, at least as a contemporary phenomenon" (quoted in Hellwig 199:131). Frazier's remark was an astute one. Although recent affirmative action policies, initiated by Brazil's former president, Fernando Henrique Cardoso, provoked an unprecedented national debate about racism in Brazil, the relative dearth of everyday discourses about systemic racism continues to the present day.[1] Among middle-class Brazilians particularly, talk about race has tended to emphasize the notion of democracia racial, or racial democracy—the belief that Brazilians have largely avoided the racialized prejudice and discrimination that characterize nations such as the United States. In such an ideological context, the silence surrounding the subject of racism is typically read as evidence for the idea that color does not play a significant role in the organization of social relations in Brazil.[2]

This chapter is based on a twenty month period of ethnographic research in Rio de Janeiro that extended from 1990 to 1992. My research predates the introduction of affirmative action policies by a decade, and it examines silence in cultural and discursive arenas distinct from those in which more recent, public debates have effloresced. Although the attention given to competing conceptualizations of race and racism in governmental and university settings as well as the news media has indeed been remarkable and deserves the scrutiny of scholars (Htun 2004), I am concerned with the quotidian spaces, the ordinary, everyday arenas in which we might examine the play of silence surrounding racism in Brazil. Although this silence has been anecdotally noted by other scholars studying the issues of race and racism in Brazil, it has not been systematically explored—perhaps because patterned silences themselves have received little attention in the anthropological and sociolinguistic literatures. In a previous publication (Sheriff 2000), I have presented an analysis of the ways in which three groups—poor African-Brazilians, middle-class whites and black militants—conceptualize and account for the notable lack of everyday discourses about racism in their nation. Here, I will briefly reiterate the central arguments of that article and pursue an additional means of understanding silence: a symbolic analysis of the legend of Escrava Anastacia, a popular saint who is said to have been a slave woman who "died for her people." I argue that the figure of Escrava Anastacia—a figure well known to my poor African-Brazilian informants—derives much of its power from its ability to symbolically represent the silencing of discourses about racism. Anastacia's story, and her image, emphasize the concept of the "muzzling" of speech and as such, they support my contention that the silence surrounding racism does not represent a mere lacuna within discourse but constitutes a form of cultural censorship that speaks volumes about the racialized distribution of power in Brazilian society.

Racism and Silence in Brazil

With a non-white population estimated to be anywhere from 40 to 70 percent, Brazil has the largest African-descended population outside of the countries of Africa. Brazil's early economy was powered largely by slave labor and the production of export crops. Partly in response to the increasing restiveness of the slave population, slavery was finally abolished in 1888. Brazil's race relations, both past and present, have been publicly constructed through the ideology of democracia racial, or racial democracy, a set of beliefs and discourses that maintain that racialized prejudice and discrimination are especially mild or even non-existent in Brazil. Democracia racial has its roots in the discourses of Brazil's slave-owning elite; they maintained that the quotidian relations that constituted slavery in their country were "softer" and more "benign" than the ostensibly more rigid beliefs and brutal practices that characterized the institution in North America (Harris 1964; Skidmore 1993). As a set of public (and inherently nationalist) discourses, democracia racial was fully codified by the 1930s, when Gilberto Freyre, Brazil's preeminent sociologist-historian published Casa Grande e Senzala (translated into English as The Masters and The Slaves, 1986 [1946]), his classic description of what he called the "New World in the Tropics." Largely through his assertion that Portuguese and Portuguese-descended slave owners were erotically drawn to black and indigenous women, Freyre argued that Brazilian culture was a true melting pot, constituted by a promiscuous intimacy between European, African and Indian "races." Within everyday discourses, Brazilians continue to echo Freyre's pronouncements about Brazilian culture, particularly his assertions that there has always been intimacy between whites and people of color rather than distance, that most Brazilians are "racially mixed," and that Brazil is relatively free of the racialized forms of prejudice and discrimination that plague countries such as the United States.

Scholars working in several disciplines began to critique the notion that Brazil is a racial democracy as early as the late 1950s. The issue has been revived more recently and has continued to generate both interest and contention, particularly over the last decade. Among North American scholars, however, there seems to be something approaching consensus regarding the mystificatory character of the varied discourses and images that constitute democracia racial (Andrews 1991; Burdick 1993, 1998; Butler, 1998; Dzidzienyo 1971; Fontaine 1985; Goldstein 1999; Hanchard 1994, 1998; Sheriff 1999, 2000, 2001; Skidmore 1993; Twine 1998; Winant 1992). Brazil's distribution of wealth is one of the most inequitable in the world, and it follows a racially bifurcated pattern. People of color remain concentrated at the bottom of the socio-economic hierarchy; they suffer higher rates of unemployment and underemployment, higher rates of disease and infant mortality, lower levels of education, lower wages, and shorter life spans than do whites (Hasenbalg 1979, 1985; Lovell 1989; Silva 1985; Wood and Carvalho 1988; Wood and Lovell 1992). Although many Brazilians as well as an earlier generation of social scientists (see especially, Wagley 1963) have argued that such inequality results from the discriminatory practices and cumulative disadvantages associated with class, research convincingly demonstrates that specifically racialized forms of discrimination also play a significant role in the structuring of inequality in Brazil (see especially Hasenbalg 1979, 1985; Silva 1985; and Wood and Carvalho 1988).

Despite the pervasiveness of practices and discourses that denigrate and de value blackness, anti racist movement and activism have been highly attenuated in Brazil. Black movement organizations are small and disorganized and many Brazilians, at the time of my research, remained unaware that such movements existed (Hanchard 1994; Sheriff 2001).

Between 1990 and 1992, I conducted ethnographic research in Rio de Janeiro in order to investigate how the contemporary meanings associated with race, racism, and democracia racial are culturally constituted. Because I was particularly concerned with the extent to which poor Brazilians of African descent defined, experienced, and interpreted racial meanings and racism, and how they articulated their stance toward the ideology of democracia racial, I lived in Morro dos Sangue Bom, a favela, or shantytown, located within Rio's city limits. In the early 1990s, Morro do Sangue Bom was inhabited by approximately five thousand residents, the majority of whom were of African descent. I expected to find something like the "hidden transcripts," that Scott (1991) has proposed, a set of counter hegemonic discourses that emphasized the prevalence of racism and that contradicted the claims that denied its existence.

As I have discussed elsewhere (Sheriff 2001), notions of race and color and the complex vocabulary associated with them figure within the everyday discourses of people in Morro do Sangue Bom. Although my informants tellingly quoted the colloquialism that "if you are not white you are black," everyday conversations in the community, as elsewhere in Latin America and the Caribbean (see, for example, Godreau 1995; Khan 1993; Lancaster 1991; Martinez 1974; Segal 1993; Wade 1993) were peppered with euphemisms and diminutives whose purpose was to avoid or soften references to blackness.

While the ideology of democracia racial insists that race is not a significant (or oppositional) component of cultural identity in Brazil, people in Morro do Sangue Bom, like their counterparts of other colors and classes, routinely engage in locutions that articulate the devaluation of blackness. Comments such as "He is preto (black), but he is a really cool person," or "She is very dark, but she is a hard worker," reveal pervasive assumptions about the notion of race and its meanings. People in Morro do Sangue Bom use, and are the recipients of, racialized epithets that reference and pragmatically demean blackness; they are also familiar with, and occasionally use epithets that refer to whiteness. Despite the fact that the significance of race and racialized opposition are coded within these everyday discourses, more explicit reference to, and narrative accounts of, racism are relatively rare in Morro do Sangue Bom, just as they are within other social milieus in Rio de Janeiro.

As I discovered, the relative dearth of open discussions about racism should not be read as support for the claims of democracia racial. When I began to conduct more formal interviews with people in Morro do Sangue Bom, the vast majority narrated personal encounters with racism. "You know it's racism when you apply for a job and they tell you they have no openings," as one woman said plainly, "and then your white friend goes and gets the job." Other stories that involved what were felt to be more personal, and thus more deeply humiliating encounters were recounted at least as often, and with more emotion. I thus observed a marked contrast between the extent to which racism was discussed in ordinary everyday contexts within the community and the ability and willingness of individuals—in interview contexts—to narratively reconstruct the actions, words and private feelings that constituted their personal encounters with racism.

My informants confirmed my impression that the subject of racism was avoided in everyday conversations, even those between intimates. Very few adults could recall overhearing or participating in conversations about the issue that might have occurred during their childhood and many parents I spoke with told me that they did not discuss racism with their children. Many of the stories about racism that informants narrated for the benefit of my research had not been previously recounted to spouses, friends, or kin. "Ninguem gosta de falar," ("No one likes to talk about it"), I was told over and over.

People in Morro do Sangue Bom, it was clear, certainly recognized their own silence. Yet, unlike many of their white middle-class neighbors, whom I also interviewed, people in the favela never asserted that racism was not discussed because it was of no social or political consequence in their country. Moreover, they never called upon Brazil's history of state-sponsored repression and censorship as a way of accounting for what some vaguely referred to as a "fear" of speaking openly about racism. In the 1950s, Getulio Vargas, Brazil's populist dictator outlawed the few nascent black consciousness organizations then in existence, and in the 1960s and 1970s, university professors were widely believed to have been exiled at least partly in response to their published critiques of racism (Skidmore 1985: 16). Nevertheless, the relationship between political censorship and cultural censorship appears to be an indirect, rather than a causal one. Such events, even at the time of their occurrence, evidently remained distant from the quotidian concerns of impoverished and politically marginalized Brazilians such as those living in Morro do Sangue Bom. Moreover, the widespread cultural reticence in discussing racism existed prior to the repressive regime (Hellwig 1992) and until affirmative action policies were officially endorsed in 2001 it has remained largely unabated throughout Brazil's democratizing process. These facts, along with my effort to under-

stand how people in Morro do Sangue Bom themselves account for and experience silence (particularly that which is observed in private contexts in which surveillance would, at any rate, be impossible), suggest that explanations must be sought elsewhere.

Accounting for Silence in Morro do Sangue Bom

As I have noted, the vast majority of my informants in Morro do Sangue Bom recounted stories about their personal encounters with racism for the benefit of my research. I often asked them why they had not told these same stories to those with whom they were intimate—spouses, parents, siblings, or friends. One of the briefest but most provocative responses came from Guillerme, a man in his early twenties. Like other men living in the favela, Guillerme was targeted as a supposed "suspect" while he was traveling on Rio's city buses. In the Brazilian version of racial profiling, young black men are often ordered off the bus, frisked, and interrogated. After describing one such incident, Guillerme noted, "It was because I was the only black person on the bus." When I asked Guillerme why he and others in the favela rarely spoke of such incidents, he told me, "Oh, well, people want to forget and let it pass. That's why people don't talk about it. It's a form of forgetting, of trying not to remember."

As Guillerme's intriguing response makes clear, the relative silence surrounding racism in Morro do Sangue Bom is not perceived as a mere absence of talk. Cultural censorship involves a degree of agency, for it is a "form of forgetting," or more precisely, it is a practice that is directed toward "trying not to remember." The suppression of discourse, as Guillerme's comments suggest, has both private and collective dimensions; it is psychologically as well as culturally and politically motivated. Guillerme continued,

> It doesn't do to keep talking about it. It doesn't resolve anything. It doesn't change things. If racism comes from the big person, right, on top, well, it's hard for the person on the bottom to say anything.

Significantly, Guillerme's abrupt shift between the issue of talking about racism among intimates such as friends and family members to the imagined scenario of talking back to the "big person," the powerful white racist, occurred in the responses of many people in Morro do Sangue Bom. Jonas, for example, another young man in his twenties, told me a wrenching story in which a white acquaintance urged him to apply for a job with a firm that was seeking to hire a man with Jonas's skill level. Jonas went to the firm but was told there were no openings. Later, his friend informed him that he had belatedly discovered that the firm had an unwritten policy of not hiring blacks. Infuriated, Jonas went to the police station to report the incident, for such discriminatory practices are a crime in Brazil. "I arrived there crying, crying, crying," Jonas told me. A police officer offered him a glass of water and said to him, "Don't get hotheaded, no. Just let it go" (Não esquenta a cabeca, não. Deixa pra la). As Jonas told me, "nothing was resolved."

When I asked Jonas if his friends in the community tended to recount similar experiences in the course of everyday conversations, he replied, "Some tell what happens, some don't tell. It's like I already told you, the subject is rarely touched on but I believe [racism] exists." Despite the fact that Jonas understood that my questions referred to talking about racism between status equals, he turned, as others had, to the impossibility of talking back in public, oppositional contexts:

> There isn't a way for it to be resolved. If someone mistreats me because of my color, am I going to punch him? I can't do that. You just have to let it go. Let it go, right, let it go (deixa pra la). You can't even—you can't lose your temper (esquenta a cabeca) over it. You forget what's happening. It passes. I let it go. I think this is the best way of resolving it.

As Jonas and others in Morro do Sangue Bom knew, the threat of punishment that one would face for talking back is very real. This fact would seem to offer a powerful explanation for the silence—indeed, political repression—which is primarily constituted by the constant arbitrary police harassment that occurs in today's war-torn Rio, exists as a constant backdrop to silence and the kind of self-conscious complacency and passivity described by Jonas. Nevertheless talking back, and talking about (particularly, but not exclusively, in the sense of self-disclosure) remain very different acts that occur in very different contexts. While my informants seemed to discursively draw the two together into one explanatory web, they certainly recognized the distinction between them.

How is it that the myriad forms of social and political repression that people suffer in the public arena bleed into the sequestered, and in many ways, protected, private space of the shantytown community and the familial households within it? What is the relationship, in other words, between those forms of silence which (at least potentially) involve force, coercion, and threats, as well as dramatic differences in the power of opposing interlocutors, and those forms of silence that are not explicitly coerced and that are practiced by status equals? A part of the explanation may reside in the experience of vergonha, or shame.[3] Although people in Morro do Sangue Bom recognize the connection between the practices associated with racialized discrimination and poverty, many of my informants emphasized more directly interpersonal forms of racism (which often involve the use of racialized epithets) and their private feelings of intense humiliation. This humiliation appears to be closely aligned with the experience of vergonha.

When I asked Robertson, a young man of twenty, why people rarely told their family and friends about encounters with racism, he suggested that vergonha may play a role in people's decisions to maintain silence:

> Perhaps they feel ashamed over their suffering. They withdraw themselves with vergonha. Or perhaps when you suffer over something, you don't want to tell people, you don't want to explain, because you're afraid that afterwards, people will treat you the same way. They might think it's your fault.

Robertson's explanation is a chilling one, but the concept of shame is one that is repeatedly invoked in efforts to explain the silence of victims of certain kinds of violence, particularly rape and spousal abuse. As is the case with rape, everyday discourses about racism in Brazil sometimes imply that the victims of racist assault (whether constituted by symbolic or physical violence) have somehow provoked their attackers. A woman in her fifties who spoke articulately about institutionalized racism in the public sphere, for example, nevertheless responded to my question about her own experience by saying:

> I, at least, have always gotten along with white people. I was never discriminated against.... So, that's how I am. I have always tried also to learn and to give. There really are dark people who are very discriminated against when they're badly behaved, when they have no manners. So they become discriminated against.

The association between vergonha and encounters with racism was corroborated by other informants who described their attempts—made during childhood or adolescence—to discuss racism with their parents or friends. Their efforts to seek comfort and reassurance after an encounter with racism were often rebuffed. Their accounts might be met by silence, dismissive gestures, or the suggestion that they had been subjected to

racism because they were badly dressed or ill-behaved. Such exchanges, I believe, may contain levels of meaning and degrees of ambivalence that are extremely difficult to untangle. Dismissive locutions may, in some cases, be directed less toward the victim and his or her experiences than toward the implicit claims within racism itself; what is being denied is not the existence of racism so much as the notions of inferiority that racism articulates. Regardless of the intentions behind these dismissive responses to narratives of racism, the effect is to discourage further self-disclosure and discussion.

The experience of vergonha and the possibility that it may be exacerbated rather than relieved by talking about racism is no doubt only part of the explanation of the silence surrounding racism in Morro do Sangue Bom. I believe the answer to this question is also powerfully conveyed in Guillerme's reference to silence as "a form of forgetting, of trying not to remember." My own culturally constructed notion that painful emotions lead to a desire to "unload" those emotions by talk—and that such talk might lead to more directly political forms of engagement—seemed to hold no sway in the community. As many of my informants insisted, dwelling on racism serves no constructive purpose. If concrete amelioration cannot be expected, they seem to suggest, then there is no point in discussing the issue. Talking about it, in fact, only magnifies feelings of anger, humiliation, and sadness. As Jonas told me, maintaining silence in the midst of a humiliating racist attack helps one to "forget what's happening." The dissociative impulse, the will to remove oneself from the immediate rage of the encounter crosses the boundary from public to private where it is maintained, after the event, as a will to erase memory – if not in a literal, then in a figurative sense. This impulse, however, is neither "unconscious" nor "pathological" in the sense defined by the psychology of repression but is collective and contractual in nature and, my informants insisted, consummately practical. The silence surrounding racism is a conscious practice directed toward the communal management of emotion.

In Morro do Sangue Bom, the will to "try to forget" about racism and to "let it pass" is clearly compounded by a general sense of hopelessness. Most of the people I spoke with in Morro do Sangue Bom offered the view that "racism will never end." Yvonne, a woman in her late twenties, articulated what I believe to be a set of widely held sentiments about the futility of talking about racism even among one's intimates:

> No, [people] don't converse [about racism]. I think they don't feel unsettled by it, I don't know. I don't know how to explain well why not, you know? I think it's a

> little like that – there's no way to change things. Accommodation, right? There's no way to change things, it doesn't help, you know? [People think to themselves,] "I'm not going to get ahead," right? It is fear also, you know, fear of competing with the white. I think it's accommodation, fear, a lack of hope, of faith, of not believing in oneself, right? [People think to themselves,] "I can, I am able, I'm going to go out there, but I'm not going to succeed." It's a lot of that.

Yvonne's comments, like those of others in Morro do Sangue Bom, account for non-coerced silence in primarily psychological terms. Yvonne's reference to "accommodation" appears to invoke a political interpretation of cultural censorship. While a collective acquiescence is implied by both silence itself and informants' accounts of and accounting for silence, I believe that what Yvonne and others refer to is a more private kind of psychological accommodation—an accommodation that is primarily determined, obviously, by the seeming intractability of the structural and cultural force of racism and the social, political, and economic vulnerabilities that it produces for people such as those in Morro do Sangue Bom. Their practice of cultural censorship appears, ultimately, to be directed toward protecting oneself and one's intimates from protracted anger and the festering of emotional pain.

Silence and Sainthood: The Legend of Escrava Anastácia

Although silence seems to be constructed and maintained through unexpressed understandings and is indexed in discourse—particularly in expressions such as "let it go," "it doesn't help," "don't get hotheaded," and "don't concern yourself with it"—it appears to be, relatively speaking, unmarked and unremarked. It is as though silence itself, the act of "trying not to remember," is buried in a kind of forgetting. While the metaphor of psychological repression seems to offer itself at this juncture, it is not a truly apt one, for people in Morro do Sangue Bom know very well that racism is pervasive and wounding—their forgetting, in this sense, is unsuccessful. Still, if silence is meaningful, we might expect it, much in the manner of repressed material, to surface or to be marked, in however displaced a fashion, in genres other than everyday discourse. I believe that the story of silence is, in fact, represented in the figure of Escrava Anastácia, a popular saint whose image and mythical biography are well known in Rio de Janeiro.

I first became aware of Escrava Anastácia (or Slave Anastácia) very early in my fieldwork. Her image is reproduced on placards, religious pamphlets, wall hangings, religious medals, and in the plaster busts that are sold in Rio's religious shops. While Anastácia is believed to bestow mercy on her devotees, there is nothing gentle in her image. She is always portrayed from the neck up. She has the short, tight hair, dark skin, and broad nose of a negra. When she is represented in color, as in the plaster busts, her eyes are blue and they are said to be "very penetrating." Her neck is encased by a thick iron collar and her mouth is choked by an iron muzzle, a device that is called a mordaça. As her name implies, Anastácia was a slave woman and as her image unambiguously reveals, she was a victim of what were once conventional methods of punishment and torture.

The origin of the Anastácia legend is clouded in controversy. The image of Anastácia seems to have originated in an illustration of an anonymous slave drawn by the French artist M. J. Arago, who traveled to Brazil in 1817. Beginning in 1971, Arago's illustration was exhibited in the Museu do Negro (housed in the Igrega do Rosario, a traditionally black church) in Rio de Janeiro. The director of the museum, a man by the name of Yolando Guerra, evidently had a vision about the illustration and began to elaborate what later became the biography of Escrava Anastácia. This, at any rate, is the account given by church authorities who investigated the Anastácia legend. In 1987 they concluded that Anastácia, also called Santa Anastácia, or Saint Anastácia, never existed. Her image was removed from the Igreja do Rosario, much to the consternation of a number of my informants. Aware of but unmindful of the church's pronouncement, devotees of Anastácia now congregate at a temple dedicated to her in Maduriera, in Rio's North Zone.

I am not concerned here with the controversy surrounding the popular saint, nor with the religious beliefs and practices that are associated with Escrava Anastácia.[4] While living in Morro do Sangue Bom, my concern was with the ways in which informants narrated the story of Anastácia and how they explained the presence of the mordaça, or muzzle, in which she is depicted.

Like all popular saints, Anastácia is believed to intercede for those in dire need and to perform miracles for her devotees. More than a few of my informants told me that they believed in Anastácia; they had addressed many prayers to her and they were answered. At the same time, however, people in Morro do Sangue Bom were aware of the fact that Anastácia's sainthood was rejected by church authorities. I asked Dona Janete, a woman in her sixties—and one of my most perspicacious informants—why this was the case. She responded with a hoot of laughter, "Oh, it must be because she is a black woman, right, my daughter? If she were white, she could be a saint but she is a preta!"

Other informants, while not professing belief in Anastácia, called her the "protetora dos negros," or the protector of the blacks, and in one case she was called a "great orixa," or god of the Candomblé pantheon. Even crentes, or Protestants, who did not believe in Anastácia's sainthood were nevertheless able to narrate at least parts of the Anastácia story. This familiarity is due, in large part, to the fact a telenovela, or miniseries, about Anastácia was aired on a major Brazilian network in 1990. There are, of course, many versions of the Anastácia story and the novela's screenwriter no doubt mixed some of the common elements from popular, oral versions of her biography (and those found in religious pamphlets) with elements from his own imagination.

Elena, a Prostestant in her fifties, declared herself immune to the claims of Anastácia's sainthood but she recapped the novela with considerable enthusiasm. Her narration contains most of the elements I heard in other informants' accounts and thus serves as a template:

> Escrava Anastácia was a slave who they say was sacrificed. She was a really beautiful slave woman, really black with blue eyes. She was enslaved by a plantation owner. He put her to doing really brutalizing work, you know? But she did it without complaining. But he wanted her, wanted her as a woman. She didn't want that, no way. So her put her in the stocks and flogged her.
>
> The people in the slave quarters were her friends. She was the leader of the slaves. Anything that had to be done, she was always in front. If, for example, there was a sick person, she went to them to lay on hands and cure them. So out in the slave quarters, she helped the negros.
>
> When the [plantation owner] saw that she didn't want to be his woman, he said, "Fine, you're going to take care of my children. I'll give my children a black doll with blue eyes." So, she took care of the children but he kept bothering her. So, he said, "Since you don't accept me, I'm going to do something so that you will never again speak in your life." So he put an iron collar on her neck and an iron mordaça, squeezing her mouth and nose. I mean, because she was always helping her people, he would really enslave her, so she would never speak again. So, she stayed that way and continued to take care of the children, without ever speaking.
>
> She was getting sick and the plantation owner called a doctor. The doctor told him to take the collar and mordaça off her. She said, "Put it back on. My hour has come." The doctor put it back on because there was nothing more he could do for her.
>
> So, the plantation owner's son was tubercular. He was complaining, crying in pain. So the man came, the plantation owner, who put the collar on her. He kissed her hands and said, "For the love of God, save my son's life. I don't want to lose my son." She put her hand on [the boy's] head and passed her hands over him very slowly. Once she got down to his feet, she took her hands away and

> closed her eyes. The boy got up and called his parents. Then everyone said, "Thank God, thanks to Anastácia, my son is cured!" So everyone was happy. But they could do nothing more for her because when she finished curing him, she closed her eyes and died.

In Elena's narrative Anastácia was "sacrificed" both because she rejected her master's advances and because she was a leader to "her people," the slaves who shared her burdens on the plantation. As Elena had, most people who talked to me about Anastácia touched on both of these elements, although some emphasized one over the other. Perhaps predictably and logically, a few of my informants provided versions in which it was suggested that Anastácia did not succeed in repelling her master's abuse; she was raped, yet remained proud to the end. (See also Guillermoprieto 1990: 179). In such accounts, stoicism in the face of violation is emphasized. Other informants, however, emphasized not Anastácia's victimization but her heroism. Although Jorge, a man in his thirties, expressed doubt about popular saints in general, his attempt to narrate the story of Anastácia was emotional:

> I don't understand it well, I don't understand her story well. I saw a little on television. Anastácia. She was a protector, right? She was a saint. She was a woman who died muzzled (amordaçada), for her people. For her race. God! I mean, she was a person who died for her race! You understand, she died for her race. That guy took the mordaça off and it was pure gangrene in her mouth. She died from that. Why? To defend her people, to help her people. She gave her hand to her people.

When informants did not spontaneously bring up the issue of Anastácia's mordaça, or muzzle, I asked them about its significance. The word mordaça, as well as its verb form amordaçar, and its adjective form, amordaçada, were known by everyone who discussed Anastácia with me. Also called a folha de Flandres, the mordaça was a commonly used "disciplinary" device during the era of slavery. According to most historical sources, its purpose was to prevent slaves from drinking cane liquor, and/or from eating dirt.[5] Both my informants' comments and standard dictionary definitions pose a rather different purpose for the mordaça, however. The Novo Dicionario Aurelio defines the word mordaça as "An object with which someone's mouth is plugged with the end that they can neither speak nor protest (grite)." Figuratively, the word is defined as "repression of the liberty to write or to speak." The verb form, amordaçar, is defined as "to impede speech."

When I asked Yvonne about Anastácia, she did not mention the issue of her master's sexual advances or abuses. She said that Anastácia "struggled for the race, right, for the slaves, and after she died, I think that people continued believing in her." When I asked her, "What is the significance of that thing she has?" Yvonne replied, "The mordaça on her mouth, right?... Now, it is said that there are people who talk too much and it is said that she talked a lot, she really talked so.... It's because she talked so much like that he put that mordaça on her."

Other responses were similar but lacked Yvonne's hesitance. A number of people told me that Anastácia's master locked her into the mordaça to prevent her from telling others about his abuse. A man in his thirties told me, "I think she suffered because she was used as an object, her master used her like an object... . That mordaça—they say that it was so that she could not protest."

A woman in her forties told me that Anastácia had "already done many miracles" for her and she said: "It was so she couldn't tell [others] what the master did with her, you know? He muzzled her mouth.... Because of what she had gone through, she couldn't say anything to anyone with that iron mordaça on her mouth. I believe in her."

Susana, a woman in her thirties, made similar comments. She had told me that Anastácia's master tried to rape her. She resisted and he put the mordaça on her: "Because then she didn't shout. It was so she couldn't call for help. Because she was muzzled, she didn't yell, you understand? So he muzzled her so she couldn't protest and from that she died bit by bit, without food, without speaking, and without drinking, right?"

In all of these comments, the purpose of the mordaça is related to a literal muzzling of Anastácia. Specifically, it prevents her from telling others, her friends and supporters in the slave quarters, what was being done to her. In these narratives, Anastácia is muzzled not only as punishment for her resistance or outspoken leadership in the slave quarters but also so that she could not "gritar," or reveal the abuse she had suffered. Although we might expect that the master would be, in a sense, omnipotent—not required at any rate to justify or defend his actions, however brutal—his exploitation and abuse of Anastácia must be kept a secret.

Other informants also explained the logic of the mordaça in terms of the prohibition against speaking that was imposed on Anastácia, although in more general terms. A woman in her sixties said, "He didn't give her the right to express what she was feeling. He muzzled her so she had no way of speaking. She became mute."

A woman in her twenties told me, "She was a person who had a facility in speaking, for communicating messages. People believed in her prayers. And the mordaça signified a form of impeding her speech."

A teenage boy simply said, "She had power in the word. She was muzzled so she would not speak anymore." When I asked Analucia, a woman in her forties, about the significance of the mordaça, she said, "Because the mordaça prevents the person from speaking, right?.... You can't say anything of what you know and what you have heard... . I think this is what happened to Escrava Anastácia. She didn't get to tell her story."

As she had on other occasions, Dona Janete pulled the threads of these ideas together into a masterful interpretation. She had not seen the telenovela. Much to her consternation, her husband and sons were given to compulsive channel surfing on the family television. She told me that Anastácia was "sacrificed" because of her beauty; "She was killed, little by little, right?... He put on her face that mordaça, right, on her mouth." "And why did she have the mordaça?" I asked Dona Janete:

> It must have been for her to suffer from not speaking. Like, here, everyone shuts their mouths, right? So, they shut Anastácia's mouth. The first thing they did was to put that mordaça on her and she didn't speak anymore.... She had it here, around her head and everything. Meaning, the law for the negro is to really keep silent (de calar mesmo). It has been thus since slavery, right? The law for the negro is to keep silent. It began through Anastácia, right? They put it right on her mouth. Why didn't they put it some other place, around her middle, on her legs, in some other place? They put it right on her mouth.... She was sacrificed little by little and she could say nothing... . So I think it was clearly this. They put it on her so she couldn't speak of what was happening to her, and it was like that until the end of her life.

As my quotations suggest, informants' explanations of the significance of Anastácia's mordaça were remarkably consistent. My informants identified with the muzzling of Anastacia—Dona Janete made this identification abundantly clear in her comment that "The law for the negro is to keep silent." There are, however, other ways of reading the Anastácia story. For Alma Guillermoprieto, a Mexican journalist, the story is, in a fundamental sense, about the cultural erotics of race in Brazil. As she writes, "I was interested in Anastácia because her legend was explicitly concerned with the relationship between black women and white men, and while that relationship is at the center of the Brazilian universe, it is rarely addressed from the black point of view" (1990: 179).

The extent to which Guillermoprieto's brief analysis represents or comments on "the black point of view" is questionable but her suggestion that Anastácia's blue eyes imply miscegenation has recently been elaborated by Burdick (1998). It may well be that some of Anastácia's devotees view her as a "beautiful mulata"—the blending of black and white features that is so celebrated in the public discourses of democracia racial—and that the legend logically (if perhaps, paradoxically) incorporates an overvaluation of "white" characteristics. Yet close attention to the precise ways in which my informants in Morro do Sangue Bom talked about Anastácia suggests that, regardless of the implication of her blue eyes, she is viewed as a negra. People in Morro do Sangue Bom claim her as one of their own and they refer to her not as a mulata, but as a preta and a negra, and it is said that she "died for her race."

In a very different interpretation, the story of Anastácia can be read as a parable about servitude, particularly the domestic servitude of black women. Nearly all of the women I knew in Morro do Sangue Bom had worked as empregadas, or maids, at some point in their lives; most in fact worked in the homes of white middle-class families from the time they were teenagers. As I indicate in another publication (Sheriff 2001), women often describe situations in which they feel slighted, exploited, and insulted while performing domestic service for others. In many cases, these insults are directly racial in nature. Usually, domestic servants have to hold their tongues. Talking back of course, can lead to abrupt dismissal. Although Anastácia was a slave and a saint, her life was not so different from theirs.

Within such a reading Anastácia represents the picture of the (nearly) perfect servant. As Elena said, she was "put to really brutalizing work but she did it without complaining." Although abused and shackled, she "continued to take care of the children." While condemned to a slow, painful, and unjust death, she rouses herself to save the master's son just before expiring. For these generous, saintly, "feminine," and submissive qualities, Anastácia, it seems, is revered. For the dominant, she is the model of one who provides "good service" and for people like those on Morro do Sangue Bom, she suggests that long-suffering patience and subordination are rewarded in the spiritual realm. To bear one's burdens without complaint, moreover, is thought to demonstrate dignity of character.

This is, perhaps, the most ambiguous angle of the Anastácia story. On the one hand, she is revered for her resistance, and on the other, she is lauded for her ability to "turn the other cheek" and to suffer in a silence, which while forced, is maintained in dignity. Read crudely as a political parable, it could be said that the message of the Anastácia story is, "This is what happens to you when you try to resist your exploitation." What such an equation leaves out is the other message: that the dignity and humanity of the slave remain inviolable. In contrast, the master, while a monster, is a pitiable one, alienated from his own humanity.

While Anastácia's blue eyes may touch the cultural nexus of meanings associated with miscegenation and the superiority of the mulata, and while Anastácia does model the dominant vision of servitude and black womanhood, these readings do not address the most dramatic motif at the heart of narratives about Anastácia: her forced silence. Anastácia's story is far more explicitly concerned with the brutality of slavery, and by extension, with the reality of racism—and, significantly, with the silence surrounding racism. For Dona Janete, it seems, the Anastácia story is somewhat like a myth of origin. Anastácia "suffers from not speaking" and this is compared to "Like here, everyone shuts their mouths." The significance of Anastácia's torture is that it dramatizes "the law for the negros," which is "to keep silent." As Dona Janete remarks, it has "been thus since slavery."

The parallels between the Anastácia legend and the silence surrounding racism in contemporary Brazil are fairly obvious. Her silence is directly linked to the overwhelming force of domination, just as my informants' explanations for their own silence are repeatedly linked to the very real danger of talking back in encounters with racism. Anastácia's story is thus analogous to the concealment of contemporary forms of racism, which are said to be "incubado" (literally incubated, or covert); "embaixo do pano" (under the cloth); and "mascarado" (masked). All of these expressions refer to the often covert practices that constitute everyday racism as well as to the unexpressed understandings that undergird silence and the discourses of denial and erasure that characterize the ideology of democracia racial. Anastácia's story thus also enacts and depicts, in symbolic form, the social, cultural, and psychological injunctions against talking about racism even in nonconfrontational, intimate contexts. She symbolizes the wounds of racism and exploitation, as well as the muzzling that is manifest in the self-censorship of people such as those in Morro do Sangue Bom.

Like Escrava Anastácia herself, poor Brazilians of African descent are entangled in a cultural, ideological, and psychological web in which neither resistance nor resignation are ever absolute. We can not sum up their position with facile references to false consciousness, because they know the truth. (A critical point about cultural censorship is that it can conceal political consciousness but does not preclude it.) Nor can we romanticize their attachment to Anastácia and claim that it expresses solidarity and resistance, for like Anastácia, they remain, for the most part, silent about what is happening to them.

I believe that the popularity of Escrava Anastácia is due in large measure to her ability to symbolically represent both the oppression of African-Brazilians and the muzzling or silencing of their voices—their inability to talk back and talk about what is really happening "embaixo do pano," or under the concealment and obfuscation entailed in the discourses of democracia racial. From what people call her "força" or strength, and from her "penetrating gaze," she tells their story without words. Escrava Anastácia is, in the direct spiritual sense that frames her sainthood among poor people of color, one who hears their muffled "grita": their inner shout, their muted protest, the call for help that is uttered in the spiritual, if not the earthly realm. Anastacia, we might say, has been there.

Conclusion

My discussion of the symbolic and deeply compelling attraction of Escrava Anastácia, and the larger processes of the cultural censorship surrounding racism, should not be read as a global analysis of silence in Brazil. As I detail in a previous publication (Sheriff 2000), the middle-class white neighbors who live close to Morro do Sangue Bom posit a different reason for silence. Their discourses provide evidence for the remarkable durability of the ideology of democracia racial; they insist that while mild racism may exist in their nation, it is of little social, cultural or political significance. Living in highly insular worlds that admit blacks only as maids, doormen and other laborers who are constrained to remain silent in their midst, middle-class whites remain largely ignorant of the profound significance of racism in the lives of those who live in Morro do Sangue Bom. Although some of my middle-class informants were aware of the fact that discussions of racism are hedged by awkwardness, discomfort and general avoidance they nevertheless believed that the silence is a largely empty one. Gilberto, one of my middle-class white informants, pointed out that, "whites, as much as negros don't touch upon the subject" of racism. When I exclaimed that they certainly didn't, he insisted, "This is data that could even prove, right, it would prove— It's good information, right? It could prove that racism really isn't important, that the racial question isn't important."

Like most such silences, the cultural censorship surrounding racism in Brazil is deeply overdetermined, and it is produced and maintained by a variety of cultural mechanisms and social actors. While the silence itself penetrates social boundaries and thus is fairly uniform throughout Brazilian society, it is clear that different groups have profoundly divergent motivations in practicing it. The consequences of cultural censorship, moreover, are not shared equally. Poor African-Brazilians, such as those in

Morro do Sangue Bom define the phenomenology of silence as directed toward a kind of adaptation to oppression. Silence appears to be experienced as a form of dissent and defense—for it is directed against the invasion of deeply wounding ideologies into the private and sequestered spaces of the family and the community. In "letting it go," and "forgetting" about racism, people in Morro do Sangue Bom collectively contain the crippling effects that the constant narration of assault and humiliation might very well produce.

Yet, the ways in which middle-class white Brazilians have misread the silence of people such as those in Morro do Sangue Bom offers powerful testament to the fact that within the larger political arena, silence has buttressed the spurious rhetoric of democracia racial. In larger terms, silences such as those that have been historically observed in Brazil remind us of the parable of the foolish king who paraded naked before his people: culturally dominant groups remain subject to the belief that their vision of their society is one that is universally shared and correct. I would argue that the silence surrounding racism in Brazil must be understood as cultural censorship, as a deeply complex, rather than "conspiratorial" form of domination. In distinguishing it from political censorship—which involves state-sponsored coercion—I have suggested that among poor African-Brazilians, silence represents a kind of "choice," a "voluntary" behavior. This point must be emphatically qualified, however, by reference to the fact that cultural censorship is both a constrained response to, and a product of, oppression. It is an index of the fact that both racism itself and the denial of its significance constitute contradictory but highly successful forms of racial domination.[6] The literary tropes that silence is "palpable" and "pregnant with meaning" have great bearing on the attempt to understand the more subterranean, but profoundly significant, aspects of racial politics in Brazil.

I would note, finally, that the recent and remarkable institution of affirmative action policies in Brazil offers unique opportunities for the study of politically meaningful silence and the varied—and less-than-predictable—means by which it might be dismantled. As Mala Htun (2004) has perceptively argued in her analysis of these policies, grassroots activism and social science research represented the backdrop against which Fernando Henrique Cardoso mobilized inspiration and support for affirmative action, but the dramatic transformation of governmental approaches to the issue of racialized discrimination occurred largely as a result of presidential initiative. To what degree will this top-down shift alter the shape of everyday discourse about race and racism? To what degree will official, state-sponsored attention to the issue of racism dismantle forms of censorship that are more a product of a complex cultural history rather than of governmental authority? More critically, to what degree will it result in significant changes in opportunity structures for Brazilians of African descent? These questions—and a more general recognition of the role of silence in shaping the socio-political landscape—merit the attention of a new generation of scholars.

Notes

Acknowledgements: Parts of this chapter have been adapted from my book, Dreaming Equality: Color, Race and Racism in Brazil, Rutgers University Press 2001. I would like to thank Charles Wood and the Center for Latin American Studies at the University of Florida, Gainesville for the opportunity to present and discuss a version of this chapter. The research on which this chapter is based was supported by a grant from the Wenner-Gren Foundation for Anthropological Research.

1. Fernando Henrique Cardoso, Brazil's president from 1995 to 2002, holds a doctorate in sociology and his early academic career was based on research on slavery and race relations in Brazil. Beginning in 2001, he initiated a variety of affirmative action policies, the most significant being the endorsement of racial quotas for civil service jobs, contracts and university admissions. In her account of the development of affirmative action policies in Brazil, Mala Htun (2004) emphasizes Cardoso's presidential initiative but also cites the activism of "issue networks" (composed primarily of black movement militants and social scientists) and the World Conference on Racism in Durban (2001) as the most significant factors leading to these dramatic policy changes. Htun notes that these changes provoked "lively exchanges in the society and the press," (2004:72) but a more precise account of shifts in the everyday conversations of ordinary, working class people such as those who populate Brazil's shantytowns and working-class neighborhoods awaits further research.
2. There are indications in recent scholarly literature that the cultural censorship of open discussions of racism may be, to obviously varying degrees, a problematic in other countries of the African Diaspora. References to the suppression of discourses that critique racism can be found in Andrews 1980; Friedmann and Arocha 1995; Fernandez 1997; Rahier 1999; and Wade 1993. The lingusit, Etter-Lewis (1991) provides a brief but provocative account of the suppression of discourses about racism and sexism among African-American women. Although the silences surrounding racism in the African Diaspora are clearly shaped by the unique histories and cultures in the local arenas and nations in which they are situated, their continuities merit

scholarly attention. In somewhat related terms, in a recent edition of American Anthropologist, Eugenia Shanklin (1999)has perceptively argued that North American anthropologists, as a professional group, have been relatively silent about race and racism, particularly in their teaching activities.

3. In his attempt to analyze the role of shame in the construction and maintenance of class-based domination, the psychologist, Philip Lichtenberg (1996) has argued that the rage produced by oppression becomes introjected as shame. Franz Fanon (1967) made a similar point years ago in his penetrating but under-appreciated analysis of the psychological correlates of colonialism.
4. See Burdick 1998 for a detailed account of the beliefs and practices associated in the legend of Anastacia in Rio de Janeiro. Burdick contextualizes devotion to Anastacia within the broader arena of gender and racial politics and their articulation with religious practice and belief.
5. The eating of dirt, evidently common among Brazilian slaves, was believed to be motivated by a desire to commit suicide by slow degrees. It was more likely caused by pica, a nutritional disorder.
6. Developments beginning later in the 1990s suggest the possibility, however, that the cultural censorship surrounding racism in Brazil may be undergoing a process of erosion in ways unrelated to the more recent institution of affirmative action policies. Research in the fields of linguistics and musicology suggests that the music and discourses of transnational hip-hop have begun to penetrate the youth culture of Rio de Janeiro. These discourses articulate not only more explicit conceptions of black identity but just as critically, explicit critiques of racism in Brazil (Ellison 1994; Pardue 2004; Roth Gordon 1999; cf. Sansone 2003). The 1996 inauguration of the popular magazine Raca Brasil, which is explicitly marketed to Brazilians of color, has evidently been instrumental in provoking more open discussions of racism. Referring to the enthusiasm with which Brazilians of African descent have purchased, read and commented on the magazine, its editor, Aroldo Macedo has said, "It's as if they had a hand over their mouths and sombody's taken the hand away. They have so much to say" (Schemo 1996:13).

References Cited

Andrews, George Reid. 1980. *The Afro-Argentines of Buenos Aires, 1800-1900.* Ann Arbor: University of Wisconsin Press.

______ 1991. *Blacks and Whites in São Paulo, Brazil 1888-1988.* Madison: University of Wisconsin Press.

Burdick, John. 1993. *Looking for God in Brazil: The Progressive Catholic Church in Urban Brazil's Religious Arena.* Berkeley: University of California Press.

_____ 1998 *Blessed Anastacia: Women, Race and Popular Christianity in Brazil.* New York: Routledge.

Butler, Kim. 1998. *Freedoms Given, Freedoms Won: Afro-Brazilians in Post-Abolition Sao Paulo and Salvador.* New Brunswick: Rutgers University Press.

Dzidzienyo, Anani. 1971. *The Position of Blacks in Brazilian Society.* London: Minority Rights Group.

Ellison, Katherine. 1994. "Feminist Singers Takes on Rap, Racism in Brazil." *The Times-Picayune*, July 17, 1994, page A24.

Etter-Lewis, Gwendolyn. 1991. "Standing Up and Speaking Out: African American's Women's Narrative Legacy." *Discourse and Society* 2(4): 425-437.

Fanon, Franz. 1967. *Black Skin, White Masks.* New York: Grove Press.

Fernandez, Nadine. 1997. "Race, Romance and Revolution: the Cultural Politics of Interracial Encounters in Cuba". PhD Dissertation, Department of Anthropology, University of California, Berkeley.

Fontaine, Pierre-Michele, ed. 1985. *Race, Class and Power in Brazil.* Los Angeles: University of California Press.

Freyre, Gilberto. 1986. [1946] *The Masters and the Slaves: A Study in the Development of Brazilian Civilization.* Samuel Putnam, trans. Berkeley: University of California Press. [Second English-Language Edition, Revised.]

Friedemann, Nina de and Jaime Arocha. 1995 "Columbia." In *No Longer Invisible: Afro-Latin Americans Today.* Minority Rights Group, ed., 47-76. London: Minority Rights Group.

Galen, Joseph. 1992. "Plane Tress and Sparrows from France: Creating Argentine Race, Nation and Civilization." Paper presented in the Annual Meeting of the American Ethnological Society, Santa Monica, CA.

Godreau, Isar. 1993."Where is Race in this Gumbo? The Slippery Semantics or Semantica Fugitiva in Puerto Rican Race and Color Talk." Paper presented in the session "Black Is, Black Ain't," Annual Meeting of the American Anthropological Association, Washington, D. C.

Goldstein, Donna. 2003. *Laughter Out of Place: Race, Class, Violence and Sexuality in a Brazilian Shantytown.* Berkeley: University of California Press.

Guillermoprieto, Alma. 1990. *Samba.* New York: Alfred A. Knopf.

Hanchard, George Michael. 1994. *Orpheus and Power: The Movimento Negro of Rio de Janeiro and Sao Paulo, Brazil, 1945 - 1988.* Princeton: Princeton University Press.

Hanchard, George Michael, ed. 1999. *Racial Politics in Contemporary Brazil.* Durham: Duke University Press.

Harris, Marvin. 1964. *Patterns of Race in the Americas.* New York: Walker.

Hasenbalg, Carlos A. 1979. *Discriminação e desigaldades raciais no Brasil.* Rio de Janeiro: Graal.

_____ 1985. "Race and Socioeconomic Inequalities in Brazil." In *Race, Class and Power in Brazil.* Pierre-Michele Fontaine, ed., 25-41. Los Angeles: University of California.

Hasenbalg, Carlos A. and Nelson do Valle Silva. 1990. "Raça e opportunidades educacionais no Brasil." *Estudos Afro-Asiáticos* 18: 73-91.

Hellwig, David J.1992. *African-American Reflections on Brazil's Racial Paradise.* Philadelphia: Temple University Press.

Htun, Mala. 2004. "From Racial Democracy to Affirmative Action: Changing State Policy on Race in Brazil." *Latin American Research Review,* 39 (1): 60-89.

Khan, Aisha. 1993. What is a "Spanish": Ambiguity and "Mixed" Ethnicity in Trinidad. In *Trinidad Ethnicity.* Kevin A. Yelvington, ed., 180-207. Knoxville: University of Tennessee Press.

Lancaster, Roger. 1991. "Skin Color, Race, and Racism in Nicaragua." *Ethnology* 30 (4): 339-355.

Lichtenberg, Philip. 1997. "Shame and the Making of a Social Class System." In *The Voice of Shame: Silence and Connection in Psychotherapy.* Robert G. Lee and Gordon Wheeler, eds.269-296. San Francisco: Jossey-Bass Publishers.

Lovell, Peggy A. 1989. "Racial Inequality and the Brazilian Labor Market." Ph.D. dissertation, University of Florida, Gainesville.

Martinez, Varena Alier. 1974. *Marriage, Class and Colour in Nineteenth Century Cuba.* Cambridge: Cambridge University Press.

Pardue, Derek. 2004. "Putting Mano to Music: The Mediation of Race in Brazilian Rap." *Ethnomusicology Forum* 13(2): 253-287.

Rahier, Jean. 1999. "Body Politics in Black and White: Señoras, Mujeres, Blanqueamiento and Miss Esmeraldas 1997-1998, Ecuador." *Women and Performance: A Journal of Feminist Theory* 11(21): 103-119.

Roth Gordon, Jennifer. 1999. "Hip-Hop Brasileiro: Brazilian Youth and Alternative Black Consciousness Movements." Paper presented at the

Annual Meeting of the American Anthropological Association, November 18, Chicago, Il.

Sansone, Livio. 2003. *Blackness Without Ethnicity: Constructing Race in Brazil.* New York: Palgrave MacMillan.

Schemo, Diana Jean.1996. "Among Glossy Blondes, a Showcase for Brazil's Black Faces." *New York Times,* October 18, 1996, Section A; Page 13; Column 1.

Scott, James. 1990. *Domination and the Arts of Resistance: Hidden Transcripts.* New Haven: Yale University Press.

Segal, Daniel A. " 'Race' and 'Colour' in Pre-Independence Trinidad and Tobago." In *Trinidad Ethnicity.* Kevin A. Yelvington, ed., 81-115. Knoxville: University of Tennessee Press.

Shanklin, Eugenia. 1998. "The Profession of the Color Blind: Sociocultural Anthropology and Racism in the 21st Century." *American Anthropologist* 100(3):669-679.

Sheriff, Robin. 1999 "The Theft of Carnaval: National Spectacle and Racial Politics in Rio de Janeiro." *Cultural Anthropology* 14(1):3-28.

_____ 1999. "Exposing Silence as Cultural Censorship: A Brazilian Case." *American Anthropologist* 102(1):114-132

_____ 2001. *Dreaming Equality: Color, Race and Racism in Urban Brazil.* New Brunswick: Rutgers University Press.

Silva, Nelson de Valle. 1985. "Updating the Cost of Not Being White In Brazil." In *Race, Class and Power in Brazil.* Pierre-Michel Fontaine, ed. 42-55. Los Angeles: University of California.

Skidmore, Thomas. 1985. "Race and Class in Brazil: Historical Perspectives." In *Race, Class and Power in Brazil,* Pierre-Michel Fontaine, ed., 11-24. Los Angeles: University of California Press.

_____ 1993[1974]. *Black Into White: Race and Nationality in Brazilian Thought.* Durham: Duke University Press.

Twine, Francine Winddance. 1998. *Racism in a Racial Democracy: The Maintenance of White Supremacy in Brazil.* New Brunswick: Rutgers University Press.

Wade, Peter. 1993. *Blackness and Race Mixture: The Dynamics of Racial Identity in Columbia.* Baltimore: Johns Hopkins University Press.

Wagley, Charles, ed. 1963. *Race and Class in Rural Brazil.* New York: Columbia University Press.

Winant, Howard. 1992. Rethinking Race In Brazil. *Journal of Latin American Studies* 24 (1): 173-192.

Wood, Charles H. and Jose Alberto M. de Carvalho. 1988. *The Demography of Inequality in Brazil.* Cambridge: Cambridge University Press.
Wood, Charles H. and Peggy A. Lovell. 1992." Racial Inequality and Child Mortality in Brazil." *Social Forces* 70(3): 703-724.

PART III

Silence and the Plight of the Observer

Chapter 7

Between Silences and Culture: A Partisan Anthropology[1]

Gerald Sider

"If they had just forgotten about us, that would have been all right, because we could remind them. But if they are trying to starve us out, I don't know what we can do."

– Darryl Johnson, Mayor of Port Union, a small and declining village on the Bonavista Peninsula, on the northeast coast of Newfoundland, Fall 2000, commenting on the policies of the Newfoundland and Labrador Provincial Government.

'... all those children died in silence."

James Baldwin, commenting in the mid twentieth century amidst the anguished cries of parents of African American children, who had three times the infant mortality rate of White children, a still-enduring difference.

I

Two thumbnail-size sketches of the recently changing situation in rural regions of Newfoundland and North Carolina will serve to introduce a widespread and characteristic situation of villagers in the context of what is loosely called "globalized" capital. The conceptual tools of anthropology seem inadequate to the task of grasping these situations. The inadequacy of theory significantly constrains the strategies that can be developed for contesting new and intensified inequalities. At the core of this problem of theory and strategy are the social processes that produce and that politicize silences.

Rural Newfoundland is almost entirely composed of small, coastal fishing villages, with a handful of dispersed service and market towns. There is one major highway that crosses Newfoundland, near the northern and western coast, and a few administrative and manufacturing towns, along with the service and market towns and hamlets, are almost all strung out along this highway. The majority of the rural population is dispersed in small villages along the seacoast. These villages, from the first Euro-Canadian settlement until 1992, were dependent on the codfishery as the primary source of income.

In the 1960s large oceangoing trawlers began systematically fishing for cod, using immense nets that could haul in over fifty tons of fish a day. By the 1970s the numbers of trawlers were proliferating, and the fish-finding and net-minding electronics were becoming increasingly sophisticated. The massive catches this technology enabled helped to make the early 1980s a time of substantial and general prosperity in rural Newfoundland. Just one cod-filleting and freezing plant, on the Bonavista Peninsula between Port Union and Catalina (the locale of the first epigraph), hired almost 1,300 local people in the 1980s—just about anyone in the area who wanted a job—and ran two shifts forty-eight weeks a year, at good wages by Newfoundland standards.

This plant, and most others, closed in 1991, after the cod biomass collapsed, having been fished to commercial extinction off the coast of Newfoundland, once the most prolific fishing grounds in the world. In 1992 the Canadian government imposed a moratorium that closed down most commercial cod fishing, creating the largest mass layoffs in Canadian history. Canada began providing income replacement to the former fishers and fish plant workers.

In 1998 the former Port Union—Catalina codfish plant reopened as a shrimp processing plant, hiring 135 workers—10 percent of the former labor force, and all with over twenty years' seniority in the old plant: thus all well into middle age. The youngest had started working at the former codfish plant twenty-six years earlier. This new shrimp plant worked for fifteen or sixteen weeks a year, not the former forty-eight, and it was just barely enough work to qualify the workers for unemployment insurance payments. The same year the shrimp plant opened, the income-replacement payments to the former workers in the cod industry ended, unless they signed up for a job-retraining program, which also included some relocation assistance, and required, in order to be accepted for job retraining and to

continue to get income replacement, that you signed an agreement that you would be willing to relocate for employment anywhere in Canada.[2]

Between 1997, when the end of income replacement was in sight, and 2002, the villages of northeastern Newfoundland lost about 25 percent of their population. This still intensifying out-migration is demographically specific: it includes almost all the young adults of childbearing age, and a substantial portion, perhaps the majority, of the potentially productive labor force—leaving behind a population that is increasingly elderly; increasingly living on social assistance, old age pensions, remittances, and transfer payments; or increasingly reduced to near-minimum waged jobs in the service sector, retail sales, and tourist-industry seasonal employment or short-term government make-work projects. Schools are struggling to stay open with rapidly declining enrollments, by collapsing grades together and dropping all special programs and courses; banks and stores, including grocery stores, are closing, churches, like unused community fishing wharfs, serve mostly to be photographed by tourists, and the villages are having increasing difficulty maintaining water and sewerage plants, and keeping their streetlights on, as their taxable population moves out, abandoning the houses that they built in the 1980s, now largely unsaleable. Rural Newfoundland is going through a period of increasing demographic, economic, social, and cultural collapse, leaving behind an aging population increasingly unable to reproduce itself either demographically or socially—increasingly unable to generate not just income-producing relations but the social relations capable of meeting their own locally—or shall we say, culturally—defined needs.

Meanwhile Newfoundlanders are in strong demand as low-cost, English-speaking laborers for construction, manual-labor, and food-processing primarily in central, western, and far-northern Canada: hard jobs, often in difficult places to live, where Newfoundlanders can be hired not only at low wages but with none of the tax-revenue social costs of producing adult workers—education, health-care, municipal services. All these costs are paid in Newfoundland, not in the locale where Newfoundlanders' labor is used.

A manager of a plant in Prince Edward Island was quoted, in November 2002, as saying, "If it weren't for Newfoundlanders ... [I] would try to import migrant workers from Mexico or Central America." This reference to Mexicans, and the obvious analogies between the government-policy-driven collapse of rural Newfoundland and rural Mexico, driving a substantial portion of the population into distant labor migration, brings us to the situation in Robeson County, on the North Carolina coastal plain, at the border with South Carolina.

II

Since 1995, when the effects of the North American Free Trade Act [NAFTA] began to be felt in the rural southeastern United States, every textile assembly ("cut and stitch") plant in Robeson County has closed and moved offshore, with approximately eight thousand people, primarily African American and Native American women, who made $12 to $14 an hour, becoming unemployed by 2002. The "lucky" ones got jobs in Wal-Mart, or cleaning motel rooms, or as "home health aides" in the massive, nationwide dehospitalization of the ill and the injured, all usually at less than $6 an hour: less than $11,000 a year, after Social Security is deducted. This crucial halving of income, usually coupled with a loss of benefits, inexorably catches up with people as their material possessions irreplaceably wear out.

The major new working-class employment is almost entirely in poultry and hog packing plants. Most of this employment is given to people called "Mexicans"—undocumented workers, primarily from Mexico and Central America, but also including Pacific islanders and southeast Asians.[3] Smithfield Hams, which has one of the largest hog deconstruction plants in the world, located on the borders of the county, hires about five thousand workers. Over four thousand are Hispanics, and the proportion seems to be increasing. The plant manager of Hispanic personnel told me that about 80 percent are undocumented. The plant also, in 2002, hired about eight hundred prisoners, primarily African American men who were bussed in daily, but recently replaced these with more undocumented Hispanics.[4] At the same time, agriculture, which is increasingly intensely chemicalized and thus increasingly dangerous, has almost entirely stopped using local labor—primarily African American and Native American—and shifted to Latino labor, under conditions with nearly no safety precautions. Meat and poultry packing plants are the highest injury-rate occupations in the United States; the long-term health consequences of intensely chemicalized agriculture are not tracked, particularly as the ill and injured "disappear" back to their home country, having served out their usefulness and done the only thing that gives anyone but their neighbors, friends, and relatives any interest at all in them as human beings.

The county director of the US Department of Agriculture, the county director of Social Services, and the director of the county's Economic Development Program all told me that since 2001 there are at least fourteen thousand "Mexicans"[5] in the county each summer, of which three thousand have temporary agricultural labor (H2A) permits and the other eleven thousand or so are undocumented workers—or as they are locally called, whatever their country of origin, "illegal Mexicans."

There are about 26,000 native-born African American people in the county; about double the number of "Mexicans," and they primarily reside in or around four small villages in the county, plus one extensive neighborhood on the south and swampy southern end of Lumberton, the county seat. The poverty, decayed housing, broken playgrounds, rutted streets, and boarded-up stores of these African-American villages and neighborhoods are a stunning sight: conditions seem very much worse than in the 1960s. Having won some significant civil rights, made effective in rural areas of the southeast in the mid to late 1970s, African American people now find themselves muscled aside, replaced by people who are utterly without civil rights, who can be pressured to work under far more duress, and who, lacking rights, come without the tax-revenue costs for social services and benefits. Further, as increasing numbers of Hispanic women have started coming to North Carolina, and staying long enough to learn English, they are starting to displace African American women from even the low-wage jobs in motels, restaurants, and retail sales.[6]

African American communities in the rural southeast are not a uniform disaster. In many smaller ones a very substantial proportion of the Whites have moved out, leaving the community in the hands of an African American political elite. This elite can use its power, and its access to state and federal grants, to provide good and useful infrastructure for the community: paved streets, sidewalks, school cafeterias, town water and sewerage to the old Black neighborhoods, streetlights, and nearly everywhere new electronically enhanced police cars and police with new kinds of armaments, each car costing more than a library in an African American elementary school. In these communities run by a politically sophisticated African American town council, we find a strange situation: well-kept and solid-looking small towns inhabited by people who are increasingly impoverished—working, when they do, at jobs that pay less than the cost of their social reproduction and provide no benefits.

III

Both in village Newfoundland and in the African American communities of coastal North Carolina, we find about two decades of modest prosperity, from the mid 1970s through the 1980s, followed by decline and then, from the mid 1990s, by increasingly severe rents in the fabric of social and daily life. In both places ordinary people are now living in a context where their social reproduction is increasingly difficult, if not impossible, in that locale. In both cases also, however, a portion of the villagers—my estimate is about 20 to 25 percent—are doing better than ever before. In rural Newfoundland these are the people who own, or work on, the new crab and shrimp boats, plus a handful of others. Their wealth is displayed in their newly built large houses, new pickup trucks, motorized toys, and, above all, their new boats. In the former plantation region, the coastal-plain of North Carolina, also about a fourth of the African American rural town population is doing quite well, primarily from government employment, their businesses, plus a smattering of corporate administrative and senior educational and ministerial positions. The new brick churches announce the prosperity of some in the congregation, although many of these new churches have yet to be air-conditioned, and by noon on a summer Sunday it can become very hot indeed: the prosperity does not reach very far at all into the congregation.

In both Newfoundland and North Carolina we need to pay attention to three basic ruptures. Most visible is the spreading rupture of loss, among adults and young adults, measured by the jagged, encircling gap between what they recently had and what they now have: a broken but necessary old car here, a leaky roof there, a health-needy parent or child, or a racking toothache, in the gap between need and can. For most people this gap has emerged in the past decade—since the cod moratorium and the end of the income support payments in rural Newfoundland; since NAFTA, the changing labor laws,[7] and the new mass labor migration primarily from Mexico in North Carolina.

Then there is a second rupture, more difficult to see and more silenced, between this adult generation who were once relatively prosperous, and their parents and grandparents. These older generations mostly grew up, and built lives, in situations of far more hardship than the current generation of adults has yet known, and from which the current generation of children and the young adults just now trying to find a place in this newly constricted job market have been, to a very substantial extent, actively shielded. Just as concentration-camp survivors characteristically said little to their children about what they went through, so also it seems that many of the youngsters of today have been substantially shielded from the horrors and stresses of a more directly brutal south—the way things were, say, for much of the mid-twentieth century. Churches, schools, and occasions—for example, the Martin Luther King Jr. Day pre-parade speeches that I have listened to—seem to regale the audience with success stories.

There is a third rupture, the most stunning of all, between those who are and those who are not "making it." This rupture—and the attached silences—expresses itself in a variety of ways. In North Carolina I was deeply surprised to find that very few people in African American communities who were not directly involved could say what happened to the more than 8,000 women who lost their jobs when the textile plants closed: this included the pastors of churches they attended in some numbers. All five pastors I asked directly, four of whom I have known for years, said they did not know. The silence (for a complete lack of knowledge makes the issue unspeakable) was particularly noticeable among the newly wealthy, who were so significant in helping to finance the expansion and modernization of church buildings, while having little knowledge of what was happening in the congregation. In Newfoundland I was equally surprised to find that the government has focused all its attention on job training and relocation subsidies for the individuals who became unemployed with the closure of the codfishery, and never asked what will happen to a village, as an entity, when all the young adults move out. There are now some fiscal questions being asked, especially about the rising costs of health care for the aged left behind, and of per-pupil education expenses as the local school population declines substantially, and distance makes school consolidation impossible, but the political and official silence around the devastating social consequences of a rapid mass out-migration is almost as shocking as the intensifying problems among the remnant populations of these frequently isolated villages.

IV

In my field research on the Bonavista Peninsula, in northeastern Newfoundland, in the summers (and one fall) from 1997 to 2002, I found a widespread romanticizing, among fisher-families, of the situation of their parents and grandparents. Perhaps the severe hardships of the small, open-boat fishery had become unspeakable. What I heard was a scatter of quite specific knowledges of the pre-1960s situation, when the small-boat fishery was the predominant form, with some themes continually stressed, such as leaving home to move into a tiny summer cabin, often only a mile or three away, to be right next to the shore and the boat, for this fishery made such intense labor demands that there was no extra time at all. And these references were continually mixed with expressions of pride in how much those generations of fishers could do, with and for so little. When I started my Newfoundland field research, in 1972, adult fishermen who themselves worked in the near-shore, open-boat fishery were far more graphic: story upon story of rowing out to fish at dawn, rowing back in mid-afternoon with a boatload of fish, pitch-forking them up on the dock, and then often staggering up the hill from shore to home, so exhausted you could not recognize your own family; or youngsters shore-salting the catch, laying it out on the pebble beach or wooden racks, turning and washing it, laying it out again—old men and women still remembering how very badly their backs hurt from this work, and no one, especially no parent, could offer any relief from work that had to be done, done quickly and for very long. They understood their vulnerability, and the inability of their kin to protect them from the demands of the merchant fishery, at the same time that they understood what they and others could make themselves do. In the context of my still-present memories of these stories, what I heard twenty-five to thirty years later, from 1997 to 2002 (to put it only slightly more harshly than it may deserve) struck me as tourist stories—people I knew well, and some for many years, giving both themselves and me the tourist or television version of their parents' and grandparents' lives: "Life was hard, bye, but we did it." [Bye = boy; a term of friendly engagement.] Sure you, or more precisely they, did it, summer after summer, and I used to count the visibly missing teeth in people's mouths, like dark clumps of too-close winter tree rings, markers of one relentlessly hard and scantly rewarded season after another. But maybe, to put a more positive cast on it all, by 1997 people were wrapping silences around suffering because at least in earlier times people were still fishing, and no matter how hard it was, it was—as they would say—"some better" than the dole.

I can tell—and have told—the identical story, with a completely different surface manifestation, for North Carolina. In 1967 to 1968, when I worked in Robeson County doing civil rights organizing, I remember tobacco being handpicked. The bottom leaves on the six-foot-high plants ripen, and are picked, first. The harvest runs from mid August to mid September—a brutally hot time on the southern coastal-plain flatlands. For the first pick or two men lay on their backs on sledges, and were dragged down the rows of tobacco plants, breaking off the leaves over their faces and bodies. For the next two picks, some days later, they knelt on these sledges, partly cushioning their knees with folded burlap sacks; the last couple of picks they stood on the sledge. This was work that hurt and that left hurts. The picked leaves were hauled to the shady side of a tobacco barn, where women, children, and old men hand-tied the leaves to lathing sticks that were hung on racks inside the barn to dry: much easier, and very much more enjoyable work, for people could mix work with talk, drink when thirsty, and keep in the shade. It wasn't all fun: substantial numbers of people got serious skin rashes and health problems that were called "tobacco poison" from handling the raw leaves, but it was very much easier and better than picking.

In the late 1970s and early 1980s the Indian people got, and developed, their own museum, and they put a model tobacco shed in it, but not a model sledge. There was no need for the kids to know, several people told me; they wouldn't understand. Or maybe the point was that they would—it does not matter, for it comes out to the same self-protection of the generation that does the telling, and perhaps also the generation that is being told. In this case the Native Americans who organized the telling of their history and culture were a generation and a social class removed from those who once picked; the people who picked before mechanization made pickers first more vulnerable and then useless.

V

What we find in these stories are silences, not silence. Silences, as we have seen, construct the (or a) present both against, and different from, the past, and also, as we shall see, construct the (or a) present both within and against an impending future.

The separation of the present from the past, which is often an antagonism to the past, and also the romantic separation of the past both from its more real self and from the present, also separates the present from the future. To not tell your children about the tobacco sledge, to not tell them about the relentless struggles against material domination and unavoidable cultural humiliation—all this shelters your children, envelops them in a seemingly better world, protects them, and perhaps undermines their ability to live either in or beyond the present: I would guess that at best it makes them more self-confident, but at the same time it denies example—real-people, real-world examples of what kin and known others could and did do.

The direct connection between silencing the past, especially a past that extends decisively into the present, and reshaping both present and future, became shockingly clear by the silences of both candidates in the 2004 presidential "debates." The African American moderator in one of the debates asked the candidates what they would do about the very high rate of AIDS among African American women. Mr. Bush said something completely irrelevant about education as the answer; Mr. Kerry, only slightly more focused, returned to his plan to expand access to health care. One major source of this epidemic among African American women is the lack of free and private condom distribution programs in men's prisons, which together with the racist-driven appallingly high rates of incarceration of African American men, the stunning length of prison sentences—the longest average sentences in the world, now that the apartheid regime in South Africa has been deposed—and the fact that many prison administrations, as a matter of unannounced policy, turn a blind eye to rape, because it forms hierarchies of domination that make the prison population easier to govern: all this makes prisons a primary vector for the spread of HIV/AIDS. None of us need to be told that in the current political climate the chances are zero (or less!) that either candidate, when presented with the shockingly high rates of AIDS among African American women, would publically say that they would work to establish a condom-distribution program in men's prisons. This separation of yesterday and today from tomorrow, this specific socially constructed silence, decisively shapes tomorrow. Silences, like culture, also divide and fracture the here and the now. *The temporal perspective on silences—their relation to the past and the impending future—is an easy reach and an easy grasp. The issue of silence and divisiveness is both harder to get our hands around, and more significant. The core of the argument about divisiveness turns on the relation between culture and silence.*

VI

In a brilliant analysis of the muddles and contradictions of such concepts as hybridity, first presented at the 2003 Australian Anthropological Society meetings, Patrick Sullivan argued—in brief, and much simplified—that while people had "culture"—and culture can be a productive focus of study—there was no analytical utility to the concept of "cultures," for internal differentiation within a so-called specific culture might well be as great or greater as that between cultures.[8] Sullivan was not—not at all—making an argument analogous to the one that permeated the struggles at the United Nations and the International Labor Organization: between the rights of indigenous *people* vs. the rights of indigenous *peoples.* Many states that are willing to grant people rights are utterly opposed to the notion that peoples have rights, for the rights of peoples are regarded as limiting the sovereignty of the state. Patrick Sullivan understands that peoples, with identities and with rights, exist. What he so usefully doubts is the utility of the concept of cultures for delineating the boundaries between peoples, and the notion, implicit in the concept of cultures, of even a relative homogeneity within or amongst peoples, and with greater differences between than within "cultures."

Like most brilliant arguments, its usefulness lies more in being conceptually provocative than perfect—a framework for beginning to understand the production and reproduction of difference, and of change, in very new ways. What I find most useful in his argument, here, is the way it permits grasping connections between culture and silence.

If we start with the notion that people have culture, but not necessarily cultures, we can counter pose to this the idea that people have, or produce, or experience, silences, but not silence. Specific silences are crucial, as we shall see, to making culture shared, inclusive, and simultaneously exclusionary. It is this double life of culture, simultaneously inclusive and exclusive, but never through simple and neat separations, that is crucial to the production of both power and difference. Think, for instance, of the long historical processes that shaped the lives of African Americans in the South (and the rest of the nation as well, of course). The point here is that the incorporation of African Americans into the dominant society was fundamentally based on the modalities of their exclusion from this same dominant society. That was the work of culture.

Silences are one major way culture excludes and includes simultaneously; makes separation and difference, and contributes substantially to the production of profound inequalities across these separations. Of special importance here, as we shall see, is the breathtaking clarity of certain politically central silences—their absolutely unmistakable meanings—along with an indefiniteness so profound it makes the silences evasive, nearly irresistible.

VII

The concept of culture, along with a package of nearly identical imposed masks and illusions—race, nation, society, citizenship, civilization—all emerged and spread, more or less together, from the late eighteenth to the late nineteenth-century. They are all profoundly exclusionary, and the practice of twentieth-century anthropology has been to ignore, or conceal, the intensity and the centrality of their exclusionary functions.[9] What we

found, in the recent social history of Newfoundland and North Carolina—and of course widely replicated elsewhere—is a "core" of processual continuity in some portion of the population, a core continuity which might, with some adequacy, be described by the terms culture, society, nation, citizens, or kin groupings. This embodied core is surrounded by people whose lives are far more profoundly delineated by the chaos and the ruptures that power characteristically imposes. Between culture and chaos are slightly permeable walls, which can most usefully be termed silences. The best definition I can build for the term "silence" is that it marks the boundaries of culture, with the chaos that power and culture characteristically impose on its victims on the other side of silence.

A final story, as a basis for making these points more clear, more real, and more useful:

In 1968 African Americans and Native Americans in Robeson County were voting in substantial numbers for the first time since Reconstruction, and as the key election was then still the Democratic Primary, they were voting for African American and Native American candidates whom they had nominated to run, and who were running in local elections—the kinds of elections that really matter: school board, county commissioner, sheriff, judges, and so on. In one precinct, with a majority of non-White voters, there was a real chance that the new candidates would defeat the conservative White incumbents, and a lot of force was mobilized, in and beyond the polling place, to make sure that even running against a significant numerical non-White majority the incumbents won. In the polling place it worked like this:[10]

Black and Indian voters entered the polling place—a schoolroom—to find a long table down the middle of the room. The voting booth, where the voters marked their paper ballots, was in front of this table; the ballot box, where the marked ballots needed to be put, was on the other side of the table, behind the three middle-aged White men sitting at the table, one at each end and one in the middle, facing the voting booth. When you came in you gave your name to the man closest to the door, who checked that you were a registered voter. The man in the middle gave you a paper ballot, and you took it into the booth and marked your choices, and came out with it—as I saw repeatedly because as an organizer I was there to watch, and supposedly to help prevent the election from being stolen—and you came out of the voting booth with your ballot folded over and over, making a small dense square.

Often the man in the middle of the table reached out his hand for this marked ballot. If you gave it to him he unfolded it, slowly and ostentatiously, the voter watching with quiet intensity (most having voted for the first time, and unsure what was happening). Sometimes your ballot was unfolded until there was one fold remaining, and then the man doing this turned around and put it in the ballot box. Sometimes it was unfolded all the way, read, and then put in the ballot box. If you ignored his outstretched hand, and walked around the table to put it in the box yourself, the man at the far end of the table would sometimes call out to the person near the door, particularly when there were several Blacks and Indians waiting to give their name or to vote: "What's his/her name?" "Who does he/she work for?" and the question that still makes the hair on my arms rise, and gives me a knot in my stomach, thirty-five years later: "Who's his/her people [kin, family]?"

Listen, listen closely, as closely as if it were said to you and it was your family that was at stake, or on the stake: No one is saying they will take away your job, or your livelihood, or make trouble for you where you live, or is making any specific threat against your family. All that is actually said are three simple questions: "What's his/her name?" "Who does he/she work for?" "Who's his/her people?" If any specific or detailed threats were made it would be a far less powerful statement of domination (as well as being technically illegal), for specific threats could be evaded, denied, perhaps even challenged. It is the silences—the unspoken *and unspeakable* space between these questions and your (and the listeners) sense of what might, and could, and did, and perhaps will happen that makes these questions what they are. It is precisely the silences that speak, that dictate—for we are not talking about democracy in this polling place, but about the dictatorship of culture and silences—about the boundaries of simultaneous inclusion and exclusion. It is these silences that mark the boundary of White Southern Culture, that make the separation and the difference between White and Black, and that, most of all, include the victims by their exclusion from a culture delineated by these very specific silences.

This is not "hegemony," as Gramsci would have it—the domination of elite culture to the point of the common sense of its victims, even though few are foolish enough not to understand what the silences are saying. Nor is it, by any stretch of the imagination, a Weberian grounding of power in legitimation: the whole notion of the "legitimacy" of power is exceedingly superficial. Power characteristically works by flaunting its widely recognized illegitimacy while simultaneously insisting on its rightness. Rather, it is the irreducible and ungraspable multiplicity of all that is implied in the silences that surround and contextualize those questions asked across the faces, and more the lives, of the voters and their families that makes culture possible—culture that, as always, both excludes and includes, and more specifically culture that denies the order and orderliness that it claims to construct and represent by imposing chaos in the lives of the victims of its orderings.

Against such silences the victims of power have a limited number of options. One is an unbounded, and necessarily incomplete, compliance—unbounded because the demands of silences, being unspecified, can never be fully met; incomplete because compliance can never either ensure the satisfaction of the dominant or the safety of the dominated.[11] Another option is to counter with one's own silences: this has nowadays become the terrain of the claimant willing to fully sacrifice himself or herself, often along with family and similar others, and on that basis unstoppably more free to go almost anywhere and do almost anything, so long as it is not spoken in advance. A third, but far from final, option, one that is of particular interest here, is to make noise: to produce a disruptive and chaotic racket through demonstrations, mass defiance, disruptive civil disobedience, and other such tactics. This noise is the silence of the relatively powerless. It carries the chaos imposed on people's lives, so characteristic of power's routine, mundane operations, back to the perpetrators, spoiling their plans, denying their hopes, disrupting their orders and orderings.[12] To understand what is at stake here one must realize that this sort of disruptive noise does not oppose silence, it *is* the collective silence of the oppressed.[13]

This understanding of noise, in its most general formulation, is the lesson that the U.S. is learning in Iraq, at such enormous cost to the innocent victims on all sides. Utter power is not, ever, subjugation of the people upon whom power is imposed. The Foucault-Bush fantasy—that power is knowledge, that power creates and constitutes its victims, and that power is subjugation: making and remaking of its subjects and itself, simultaneously—is foisted on the world with extraordinary violence and near limitless destruction.[14] But it still does not work, for at the core of the relationship between power and its victims—in the butchery of Iraq, in the drama of the broken hopes for electoral success in Robeson County, in the structural rearrangements and government policies that have eviscerated lives and communities of Newfoundland fishing families and the African American working class of rural North Carolina—in all of these the relationship between power and its victims, its subjects, is shaped by the silences that are so crucial to each. Our grasp of and on these silences is thus the foundation for a partisan anthropology, sensitive both to the exclusionary and incorporative power of culture and to its limits. Call me nigger, call me Mexican, call me terrorist: whatever you do you want to exclude me and to have me at the same time. That contradiction is your doom, for it means that you can speak to me but not with me. Power is not knowledge, as the Foucauldian fantasy would have it; it is ignorance. And that ignorance, as America should have learned in Viet Nam, and now in Iraq, and from its intensifying abuse of the more vulnerable of its own population is, unavoidably, power's doom. The *innocenti* of a more optimistic, recent past had the slogan "speak truth to power." This study of silence shows that this is, perhaps fortunately, impossible.

Notes

1. An early draft of this paper was presented at the American Anthropological Association annual meetings, November 2002, in the session organized by Avram Bornstein: *Public Policy Forum: engaged, activist and applied anthropology—what is to be done?* I thank the members of this panel, particularly Avram Bornstein and Kirk Dombrowski, for their comments. Gavin Smith and Maria-Luisa Achino-Loeb provided important advice for the development of this paper.
2. This intensification and demise of the fishery, from the 1960s through 2002, is closely described and analyzed in the prologue and epilogue (pp.1-58; 308-324) of my 2003 book, *Between History and Tomorrow: Making and Breaking Everyday Life in Rural Newfoundland.* Peterborough, Ont., Canada: Broadview Press. This book substantially updates the analysis of Newfoundland in the first edition, *Culture and Class in Anthropology and History: A Newfoundland Illustration* (Cambridge: Cambridge University Press, 1986).
3. Steve Striffler has a fine discussion of the mix of people who become categorized as "Mexicans" in his "Inside a Poultry Processing Plant: An Ethnographic Portrait," Labor History 43, 3 2002 August 2002. See also his forthcoming *The Triumph and Tragedy of Chicken* (New Haven: Yale University Press, 2005).
4. The use of prison labor to produce goods for interstate commerce is illegal. So, of course, is the use of undocumented workers, but as we have learned from Enron, the concept of corporate illegality points toward a range of permissible/impermissible actions.
5. The local Mexican food specialty shops have walls festooned with advertisements for fee-based remittals of money to workers' home countries. Reading—and counting—these ads shows that many workers come from Guatemala and El Salvador.
6. This situation is described in detail, and further analyzed, in the Introduction (pp. 1-82) of my *Living Indian History: Lumbee and Tuscarora Peoples in North Carolina*

[Second, Updated Edition of Lumbee Indian Histories](Chapel Hill: University of North Carolina Press, 2003).

7. While undocumented workers draw the most public attention, several scarcely noticed, but fundamental changes in labor law and practice have had an even more devastating effect on the working class. One set of laws and practices makes it easier to continually use trainee, or "temporary," workers, who get near-minimum wage ($5.15/hr) and no benefits; the other set denies unemployment benefits to workers who refuse to take minimum wage jobs—the former regulation permitted them to turn down jobs offering less than 80 percent of their prior wage. See the introduction to *Living Indian Histories* for further amplification of these and related points.
8. Patrick Sullivan, "Culture Without Cultures: Reassessing the Center in the Search for Boundaries and Borderlands." Australian Anthropological Society. Sydney, October 2003. Forthcoming (2006) in the *Australian Journal of Anthropology.*
9. Immanuel Wallerstein, in a particularly well developed analysis of the concept of citizen, from the French Revolution through the nineteenth and early twentieth-century in Europe and the United States, argues that citizenship was the fundamental framework of exclusion, and that sexism, racism, and classism were deeply interwoven—indeed shaped by—their participation in the process of exclusion from the core persons of the polity. Wallerstein, Immanuel ,"Citizens All? Citizens Some! the Making of the Citizen," *Comparative Studies in Society and History* 43, 4 (October 2003).
10. The following brief description condenses and focuses a broader descriptive analysis, which can be found in chap. 3, pp. 42-49, of *Living Indian Histories.* More: it attaches to this description a new and different analysis, focusing on the issue of silence.
11. Two exceedingly sensitive psychoanalysts, Victor Frankl and Bruno Bettleheim, who each survived extended stays in concentration camps, insisted on the incomplete and thus irreducibly arbitrary nature of the relation between power and its victims; Avram Bornstein has shown that Palestinian victims of torture in Israeli camps come to the same realization: the issue here is ultimately not so much the deficiencies of power but the logic of extreme inequality. Avram Bornstein, *Crossing the Green Line Between the West Bank and Israel.* Philadelphia: University of Pennsylvania Press 2002. See also Maya Rosenfeld, *Confronting the Occupation: Work, Education, and Political Activism of Palestinian Families in a Refugee Camp* (Stanford, CA: Stanford University Press, 2004) and Avram Bornstein, "Ethnography and the Politics of Prisoners in Palestine-Israel." *Journal of Comparative Ethnography* Vol. 30, No. 5, 2001.
12. This is a further development from a point originally made by Kirk Dombrowski, that "ordinary daily life" is not at all conceptually adequate for understanding the lives of a great many people, although it is one of the foundational notions beneath a range of other anthropological concepts that we use to study the same people for whom "ordinary daily life" is exceedingly, and perhaps increasingly, impossible.
13. This is not to imply an individualistic "weapons of the weak" perspective, such as used by James Scott. Nor is it to invoke any aggregate of individual actions, as with Scott or Stanley Elkins. Rather, the point about noise is a point about collective action.
14. For Foucault, see Michel Foucault, *Discipline and Punish: The Birth of the Prison.* Transl. Alan Sheridan. N. Y., Pantheon, 1977; for Bush, see your daily newspaper, especially the explanations of how the Iraquis would welcome us with open arms, or the staged toppling of the statue of Saddam Hussein.

References Cited

Bornstein, Avram. 2002. *Crossing the Green Line Between the West Bank and Israel.* Philadelphia: University of Pennsylvania Press.

_____ 2001. "Ethnography and the Politics of Prisoners in Palestine-Israel." *Journal of Comparative Ethnography* Vol. 30, No. 5, 546-574.

Dombrowski, Kirk, 2001. *Against Culture : Development, Politics, and Religion in Indian Alaska.* Lincoln, NE: University of Nebraska Press.

Elkins, Stanley M. 1976. *Salvery: A Problem in American Institutional and Intellectual Life.* Chicago: University of Chicago Press.

Foucault, Michek. 1977. *Discipline and Punish: The Birth of the Prison.* Transl. Alan Sheridan. N. Y.: Pantheon.

Rosenfeld Maya. 2004. *Confronting the Occupation: Work, Education, and Political Activism of Palestinian Families in a Refugee Camp..* Stanford, CA: Stanford University Press.

Scott, James C. 1985. *Weapons of the Weak: Everyday Forms of Peasant Resistance.* New Haven: Yale University Press.

Sider, Gerald. 2003. *Between History and Tomorrow: Making and Breaking Everyday Life in Rural Newfoundland.* Peterborough, Ont., Canada: Broadview Press.

_____ 2003. *Living Indian Histories: Lumbee and Tuscaroral People in North Carolina.* Chapel Hill: University of North Carolina Press.

Striffler, Steve. 2002. "Inside a Poultry Processing Plant: An Ethnographic Portrait." *Labor History* 43(3 August).

_____ 2005. [forthcoming] *The Triumph and Tragedy of Chicken.* New Haven: Yale University Press.

Sullivan, Patrick. 2006. [forthcoming] "Culture Without Cultures: Reassessing the Center in the Search for Boundaries and Borderlands" [Paper Presented at the Annual Meethings of the Australian Anthropological Society, Sydney, 2003]. *Australian Journal of Anthropology.*

Wallerstein, Immanuel. 2003. "Citizens All? Citizens Some! The Making of the Citizen." *Comparative Studies in Society and History* 43(4 October 2003):650—679.

Chapter 8

Silences of the Field

James W. Fernandez

Where the Silence Is Deafening

It is sure to be observed how apt for such a loquacious discipline our interest in silence is. For if we were silent for a moment during the hour of our panel that Wednesday afternoon in November 2000, we could have heard the incessant buzz of conversation in the hallways of the Hilton and the distant drone of pressured papers being rapidly read (to take full advantage of one's brief fifteen minutes of fame) in a score or more of meeting rooms. If we could be co-participatory in some part of these many loquacious events it would be deafening. Silence is a rare commodity at the meetings, as indeed it is in our decibel distracted modern world. Talk is what the meetings are about. If we were quiet for a moment we could have heard hundreds of our ambitious and dedicated colleagues talking, talking, talking. How challenging, in that context, and somehow instructive it was to meditate upon silence in that voluble venue and meditate again upon it here. We make here a kind of countercultural challenge to the normal ways of doing things in our garrulous, not to say prolix times, the kind of challenge to conventional and accustomed thought that anthropology in its many ways has always tried to offer. For that reason our effort to meditate about silence even to talk about it seems thoughtful beyond words.

It's not that the power of silence or the powers involved in imposing silence are unrecognized in literature and lore. The folklore archives testify eloquently to the presence of the motif of silence and the tale types in which silence is either imposed or the ability to preserve it is tested in the principal characters, whether heroes, villains or fools.[1] Silence in the human condition, because of our language capacities and also our interest in human relationships expressible through language,[2] is powerful and this power in social relations is seen most clearly in the power of shunning in religious communities and in the "silent treatment" in general. But it is present, as well, in many different smaller gestures of deliberate non-recognition and non-response, of turning a deaf ear, to the intercommunicative nature of human relations in which we are otherwise so much interested.

The Voices of Silence

However unique in the meeting's milieu this topic was and is, silence and in particular the politics of silencing have been brought to our attention in various arenas with some frequency in recent years. Michel-Rolph Trouillot's *Silencing the Past*[3] has become a now widely referenced discussion of the privileging of certain materials in the reconstruction of the past and the screening out of evidence averse to the politics of that privilege. To be sure, the silences of the historical record and the favoring of the aristocratic or elite voices have been long remarked and, indeed, the Annals School in France –with the Social History it has practiced and engendered in both Europe and America—has been dedicated to discovering the long-silent voices of the common people and the subordinate classes. These historians are often abetted in their research, ironically, by Inquisitional records of church authorities forcing confession and, in their efforts to silence heresy, listening intently to the anxious, squeezed-out voices of the populace for signs of aberrations of faith. Before the turn to Social History the silences imposed by elite history would have fallen like a leaden cloak upon the voices of a sixteenth-century Italian Miller with cosmological pretensions,[4] upon a pretending husband returning to Southern France from war in Spain and his pretending wife,[5] upon the obstreperous apprentices to an overbearing master printer and his pretentious wife[6]—just to take the classic works. Social history and historical anthropology have rescued a great deal, a multitude of previously unheard voices, from the silencing of the past.

The Predicament of Paradigmatic Privilege

Privilege seeks to impose silence except in the controlled circumstances of symbolic reversal, upon those over whom the privileged hold hegemony. It doesn't want the pretenses of privilege questioned. So silences and silencing are built into structures of privilege to bolster *its authority structure.* Most recently Begoña Aretxaga in a colloquium issue of *Anthropological Quarterly,* responding to September 11th and the subsequent War on Terrorism, has pointed out that the voluble attention to Fundamentalist Terrorism, as is now the case, should also be complemented by and be contrasted with the silencing effects of State terrorism. This state-sponsored silencing, often the condition of life in authoritarian regimes such as the Franco Regime in Spain,[7] is a terror antecedent to and causative of the Basque young people's "street terrorism" (so named by the authorities) which Aretxaga has studied among the Basques.

The silence imposed upon adversaries, would-be or active, is characteristic of any social formation anxious to promote its own interests and disinterested in complicating its own sense of reality and self-realization by paying attention to other points of view. The well known anthropologist and public intellectual of the mid last century Margaret Mead coined the term "intercommunicating cluster"[8] for groups within any professional discipline who tend to mainly communicate among themselves developing their own final and affianced vocabularies and so are disinterested in hearing, if *they are* not engaged in actively silencing, the vocabularies and associated arguments of other clusters. For better or for worse, Mead argued, this is how work gets done in the disciplines, however many efforts are made to be interclustering or interdisciplinary. There are many instances, known to practically any practitioner of any academic discipline, of the silencing by one method or another of other incompatible or antagonistic voices and vocabularies. If other "final vocabularies" are heard at all they are as quickly transposed into local terms and as often their origins "silenced." Fogelson offers the instance of the anthropologist and kinship specialist David Schneider effectively if not actively silencing the well intentioned but thoroughgoing critique of his (Schneider's) argument by another well known anthropologist, Anthony Wallace.[9] Paradigm theory[10] in the sciences and social sciences would argue, of course, given the intercommensurability between paradigms, that normal paradigm oriented science or social science is by definition practiced within self exclusive methods and vocabularies. This is necessarily so if paradigms are to achieve satisfactory and unconfused development. Paradigms in this sense are preoccupied with their internal dialogical development on their own terms. Often enough this development is surrounded by boundaries of silence or what may be equally well regarded as indifferent and untranslatable noise. The notion of paradigm development in normal science, and the associated notion of incommensurability between paradigms, is a notion that highlights the inevitability of governing perspectives and the servitude of truth value to point of view value. Silencing of other perspectives and points of view is inevitably implied. Any field anthropologist, however long he may have conducted his fieldwork, will be aware of this indenture and the silences that accompany it.

The Roshomon Effect

The Roshomon effect has been treated perceptively in anthropology[11] as a scenario by which to grasp the ever-presence of either the perspectival[12] or the plainly contradictory, or both, in informants' accounts of what is presumed to be a common experience for all. The effect takes its name from the mid-fifties Akira Kurosawa film, a film that features the varying accounts of four parties observant upon the murder of a samurai and the rape of his wife in the forest. One assumes that there are various "silencings" going on which are a cause of the quite varying versions of the event. For the ethnographer taking into account this "Effect" brings several advantages: the advantage of (1) an awareness of the suspected but unarticulated and hence silent presences of hidden and unconfessed agendas in the people actually consulted, which may be motivating their different accounts of a commonly experienced event and of (2) an awareness of how many distinctly different voices may be available for comment on any given event or belief or experience, voices that simply can not be attended to in the time available for ethnographic construal of what happened or was believed or experienced. These *awarenesses* together constitute, we might say, an ethnographic *alertness* to the considerable silence that surrounds or underlies the articulated ethnographic task.

In respect to the elision or suppression of hidden agendas (*awareness 1*): that is the situation where, as is so often the case, the ethnographer is being presented determinedly with an informant's platitudes rather than his or her underlying attitudes. If this is not constantly a condition of cooperative not to speak of companionable social life it is surely a condition of anthropological inquiring among informants who are previously unknown to one *and hence unlikely to reveal their underlying attitudes.* In respect to the many voices and the limited time problem (*awareness 2*): Sociological methods of random or representative sampling help solve in statistical terms the problem of neglected voices. But the nature of anthropological research with its emphasis on extensive and enduring participatory and open ended interaction and extended life history type consultation means

that not all informants can be listened to and many must, in effect, remain silent in the ensuing ethnographic account. These silences, it would seem, are inescapable presences (and absences) in anthropological fieldwork. In this sense, however communicative a discipline, anthropology is in fact one which, ultimately, is taking place among a multitude of silences.

An awareness of these silences, however, can strengthen inquiry by constraining over interpretation. Frankel, who has written one of the earliest and most penetrating accounts of the "Roshomon Effect" and the fallibilities of field inquiry it suggests, puts this cautious but ultimately positive view in this way. While we must assume the realist position that events, beliefs, entities, and so on exist independently of ourselves, we must also assume that we can not know them directly but must construe them.

> Our knowledge of the 'really real' is mediated by fallible perceptions and imperfect reason. Human knowledge of reality can never be either complete or certain, therefore; instead it involves selective interpretations of whatever may actually exist. Thus although we may not construct the world, we have no choice but to construe it. (15)

Frankel recognizes in her argument the degree to which a certain "tacit knowledge" about informants' credibility or believability almost inevitably prevails in fieldwork.[13]

> What does a field worker actually do at the end of a day of talking with informants?....(It's been a long day and after all one can't record everything. Besides everyone knows that that 'x' is unreliable so why record his version of things when it contradicts that of 'y,' one's best informant. Inevitably the ethnographer's own personal and professional biases are at work as (s)he writes an 'account of the accounts' of the day, creating another selective version of what 'really happened,' always trying to make sense of the data by refining, filtering, and occasionally falsifying it, however, unwittingly. (16)

The awareness of the assumptions present in this kind of "tacit knowledge" of informants' credibility and of the predetermined attention to certain voices, assumptions which are operative in those final moments of the evening construal of the day's investigative activities in an anthropological fieldwork, can yet make for better construals, in Frankel's argument. It is an awareness which, in the context of the thematic concern of this collection of paper, we would like to call an awareness of the ever presence of silence and silencing in fieldwork. It is an awareness of the so often tacit privileging of some informants' voices as credible or serviceable and the

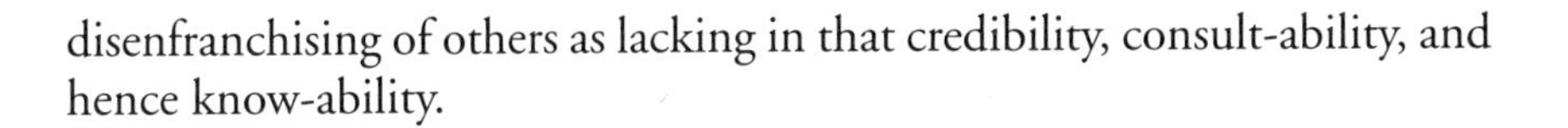

disenfranchising of others as lacking in that credibility, consult-ability, and hence know-ability.

Evocations from the Constitutive Voices of the Field

The participatory, long lasting, and engaged fieldwork of anthropologists, of course, if it is a science at all, is not a normal or paradigmatic experimental science in the Kuhnian sense. It has been, over the longest run, in the best sense a kind of Natural History in which practices of collection, presentation, classification, and comparison are, or at least were, predominant. In this task it has always been, notably, an intercommunicative science of listening, very much affected, therefore, as we have been arguing, by silence. One says "were predominant" until the postmodern period of experimental ethnography in which artful, narrative interpretation of fieldwork listening (to local narration) has replaced the Natural History tasks and has stimulated, we might argue, a special kind of listening and, as well, a special vulnerability to silence. That "special kind of listening"—with the third ear perhaps—characteristic of interpretivist and postmodern ethnography may in part account for our interest here in silence, which is a field condition of particular challenge to the attentive listener embarked on a virtuoso interpretation and hence especially attuned to virtuoso voices and their virtuoso narratives. The interpretivist anthropologist in this sense gains understanding by being aware of how many voices one has had to screen out, that is to silence, in order to listen as attentively as possible to the most interesting voices for interpretive purposes. One's understanding is advantaged by being alive to these silencings on the one hand and the menace to the enterprise of a surrounding silence on the other.

It is not, as we say, that field ethnography has not always been a matter of listening to what informants say. But in the more inquisitorial ethnography of colonial days with the anthropologist on the veranda or at "the door of his tent" armed with *Notes and Queries in Anthropology*,[14] silence was obviated by the virtually inexhaustible string of questions the anthropologist was supplied with and obliged to ask, and "the natives" obliged to answer. Native silences were squeezed into obligatory responses. I recall once quite vividly in my first fieldwork among Fang reaching an impasse of silence with informants and with no other activity to observe in village or chapel house life— I was working on "religious movement"—feeling as if I was "running out" of questions. I forthwith repaired to my hut to consult *Notes and Queries*, a great bulwark against such silence. Indeed I became known, as I have had occasion to confess elsewhere, as "nkwan minsili": "he who is sick by virtue of the number of questions he has on his stomach," that bodily locus from which questions bubbled away dyspeptically and from which their pernicious vapors were supposed to rise, often uncomfortably, into social life.

All the more, therefore, is the close listener, and thoroughgoing interpretivist and artful collector and subsequent narrator of native texts, confessions, and testimonies, challenged by the silences that can arise in the field, particularly when one does not have recourse to such an ample questionnaire as *Notes and Queries* nor a colonial situation of obligatory cooperation. And even with such a questionnaire as *Notes and Queries* the field is full of moments of anxious if not ominous silence in which the ultimate ethnography that one is going to write, itself seems threatened by the disappearance or recalcitrance of the necessary corresponding and informing voices on which it must be built.

But, of course, such anxiety arises and arose for me, for the most part, in relation to those voices on whom one was already focused, with whom one was accustomed to communicate, and upon whom one counted for the kind of fulsome account, anecdote, explanation, or story necessary to supply the corroborative detail of fulfilled ethnography. Silence in these voices for whatever reason, ranging from necessary dedication to their own tasks more important or pressing than "talking to an ethnographer" or because of some personal pique of privilege, preference, or pompousness in either party—such contretemps as inevitably arise in the negotiations of the field between informants and ethnographer[15]—these are the truly anxiety arousing silences.

These are the voices that in my own particular way of setting up ethnography I would feature upon a quasi kinship charting of the relevant others with whom I consulted; let's call them The Voices of the Field.[16] In the ethnography *Bwiti* these voices were, first, found in the *Argumentii Personae*, the chart of those thirty-eight villagers with whom my wife and I mainly worked and whose argumentative voices— Fang I quickly discovered are a very argumentative people— we mainly registered in the focal village of our study in Northern Gabon, Sougoudzapville, in which we worked. There were also subsequently indicated the forty-five voices of the "Dramatis Personae," that is to say those members of the Religious Movement, Bwiti, upon whom I was mainly concentrated and with whom I mainly consulted. These dramatic voices— dramatic because they were, after all, involved in song and dance and other dramatic activity of religious revitalization, aimed at bringing a religious world into being—were found scattered in numerous Bwiti chapels throughout the Western equatorial forest of the Gabon Republic. It was their voices I primarily registered upon my tapes or wrote down, in as verbatim fashion as possible, in my field notebooks. Returning to consult those kinship and genealogical charts today I can still evoke, however faintly, the many hours of talk spent in the Men's Council House (in respect to villagers and village life), or in the sacred and reserved chambers of the various Bwiti chapels where I studied, listening to the village debates, in the Council House, or the sermons and homilies in the Chapels and, in general, listening to and consulting with all these voices.

There were certainly many moments of trying silence even among these more regular interlocutors. Often enough when I might be launched on a line of inquiry in the Men's Council House, a sudden task in the deep forest or a hunting party would suddenly empty this interlocative place of regular rest and retirement for all villagers, leaving it to a few old and often enough barely articulate if not partially demented men. I found these oldsters garrulous and unprofitable to my inquiry although now, as I reflect back, I silenced them too quickly and might well have profited from listening to them more closely and more protractedly.

I recall being treated for the most part with the greatest patience, but from time to time my questions were of such persistence in the Council House or elsewhere that men much older than I—- I was then in my late twenties—would *silence me*, not only by humorously reminding me of my nickname among them and the impertinent and dyspeptic "sickness" that it evoked, but by occasionally reminding me that the Council House had other purposes than to serve as a chamber of European interrogation. This was a reminder almost always conveyed with humor and forbearance. Fang were a good deal less abrupt in silencing me than I, in effect, silenced some of them by deciding too early in the field whom my principal informants were going to be; a judgment made on the basis of what was mostly a tacit and too early and too easily developed measure of informant reliability and compatibility. The rest were silenced!

Pregnant Silences: *Final Notes,* Forgotten *File Notes,* Still Resonant *Head Notes*

As I revisit the argumentative and dramatic *Personae,* the constitutive voices as it were, of my ethnography and if I return and consult my field notes, several thousand pages in total,[17] I am not only still able to go beyond that over determined congregation of favorite voices and final presences, constitutive to my eventual ethnographic task, I am indeed forced by these *File Notes*[18] to go beyond them. For, as is almost inevitably the case after long fieldwork, two and a quarter years in this case in Equatorial Africa, I discover once again many more voices there noted at length or in passing than I was ever able to include in the eventual ethnography. Most of these voices had been forgotten and silenced due to the requirements of manageable ethnographic composition. But some, I see now, were silenced by accident. For, as I now reflect upon them and attune myself to them, they had something important to contribute to my understanding of Fang culture. This return to my *File Notes* brings me to hear again those silent voices and shadowy presences, presences still there awaiting me in the files, who came to be excluded in my *Final Notes* of ethnographic composition—adding if I may another notion to Sanjek and his collaborators' notions of *File Notes* and *Head Notes*. In the field one inevitably silences many voices, but that silencing also occurs in the work-up of the field notes themselves, a compendium, if fieldwork has gone well, almost always too rich in voices to be entirely included in the final write-up of the ethnography.

I can here only briefly evoke a few of these once duly noted but now subsequently lost and silent presences in the eventual emergence of Bwiti as a full-fledged ethnography. After all, the field notes accumulated in more than 800 days of Equatorial research amount to more than 1,600 single-spaced legal pages with additional maps, charts, and kinship vocabularies summing to several hundreds more. I would estimate that these volumes contain the voices of easily more than twice as many interlocutors with important things to say and observe as eventually received explicit recognition in the ethnography and its *Personae* chart. Take the case of three men whom I now recall on rereading of file notes but had long forgotten. They were articulate members of the Bwiti chapel of Abying with whom I spent a week toward the end of my research, Zame Duma Abomey, Nkoberi Nze Feh, and Yembe Oyono Mbege. I now read back through their comments on their religion, pages 685-704 of my field notes, recognizing in them now a perceptive understanding which did not, however, make its way into in any direct way *by specific reference to their voices*, into the final ethnography. Had I started my research in their villages and with them and their families they might well have been the central figures of my study and might even have figured on the cover of the ethnography, as was the case with my principal Bwiti informant, Ekang Engono. But I had started elsewhere and had already been steeped in considerable and diverse perceptive and complicated commentary on the religion. With them I think my cup risked running over and so eventually they fell silent in the final work and were of only very indirect influence on my over all interpretations. But under the prompting of our session here on silence I can go back and hear them once again. I am sure that could easily be the experience of many ethnographers.

Mintza Mve is another rather different case for he figures in my genealogical charts (1982: pages 14 and 19 and passim) and is referenced briefly a half dozen times in the ethnography. He was the eldest male member of the extended family with whom we lived *for* many, many months in our principal village of residence. But though imposing of appearance he was of a retiring temperament especially in comparison to his younger half brother, Nguema Mve, the dynamic family leader. I now recall various attempts to engage him especially as I recognized from several remarks he made in the men's Council House a special senior elder's perspective and understanding. But he did not wish to contest his brother's sponsorship of me, among other reasons, so that what I am sure would have been a valuable interlocutor for me and commentator on Fang life remained effectively silent in my eventual account.

No doubt, as I say, for most anthropologists the after-presence of many silent but forgotten voices can be easily evoked in returning to field notes. This would be true for any ethnographer with any length of time in the field, enough time to have realized how many, many voices there were to be listened to and how few he could actually attend to and who thus for various reasons had to remain silent in his subsequent work. In the case of Mintza Mve it is not only *file notes* that remind me of neglected voices once heard but now silent. For I now recall out of my still resonant *head notes*, never then written down, my feeling and my frustration that I was missing, in Mintza's retiring and resistant ways and in his usual silence in my presence, an informant of value.

Also out of my head notes I now recall the chief assistant to the charismatic prophet of the religious movement Bwiti, whom I featured on the cover of the ethnography, Ekang Engono: Michel Bie Ngounya. He is featured in the short biographies of Dramatis Personae (page 22) and is a considerable although indirect and interpreting voice in the ethnography. For the charismatic leader, Ekang Engono, was a person who cultivated his charisma through a mostly silent presence. He was resistant to speaking directly with me on any matter and insisted on employing an interpreter, in this case Michel Bie, to convey his words. His favorite place of communication was a large grave pit dug behind the altar;[19] here he otherwise spent many silent hours communing with the ancestors. There I could descend to work with him through his very able and articulate interpreter, Michel Bie. What I now recall, though I believe it is to my best knowledge in no place registered in either my Field Notes or Field Journal, is a certain unrest on Michel Bie's part in having to act as interpreter and not as central player in explaining the religion. There were also as I recall several hints given me during those weeks of his desire to meet with me alone. But as he was subordinate to the leader, no occasion arose to escape that surveillance and pass beyond his subordinate status as only the interpreter of the leader's words. So although no doubt his voice was present in his interpretations of his reticent leader, his voice is not present *as it would have been had I considered him a principal informant with a voice of his own and not simply a mediator of another's voice.* Later I heard he had left Ekang Engono's chapel and had set up his own quite interesting variety of Bwiti off elsewhere in the Equatorial forest. So his own *present but unvoiced views* for the most part were to me silent and silenced. As also in the case of Mintza Mve I was aware of a "pregnant silence." But I could not ever find or summon the possibility of midwifery, the overcoming of the *structured* silence and *enable* the encouragement of their active voices.

Conclusion: The Underlying Ironies of Our Inquiry

I don't want to forget in conclusion some of the history of "silencing" that lies behind these evocations of the various African voices to be found or recalled out of my file notes, head notes, and final notes, themselves virtually time out of time as they are. I should recognize that it was only really in the late 1950s that I or any inquirer would have had such free rein as I enjoyed to communicate with members of Bwiti about their religion. In earlier decades, until the 1950s when the more benevolent effects of the post war colonial laws protecting native rights had begun to take effect in French colonial policy, there was suppression of Bwiti and those interested in it by administrator and missionary alike. There was an active, often very severe silencing, *a repression really*, of the various voices that I had the liberty later to select among and register for archival posterity. I have written of those repressive years in the early chapters of *Bwiti*. So while I have been anxious here to tease apart and account for the presence or absence of the many different voices present in my fieldwork, my file work, my final work, and my eventual head work, I must also point out that in previous decades the colonial conditions of possibility of my particular multivocal inquiry would have been much more limited. There was *previously* much more silencing of a political nature than I encountered, the particular silences of the colonial world and the situation it fostered of unilateral communication to the natives of the civilizing mission.

In this paper I have been writing under the stimulus of our topic, silence. And silence can be as stimulating as it can be oppressing to such a communicative social animal as the human one. I have been stimulated to parse the various ways that silence was at work as a dynamic, if not a pregnant presence, in my fieldwork. Silence was both a dynamic among Fang themselves and a dynamic at work in the field as an inescapable part of ethnographic inquiry itself. We anthropologists are a discipline that depends very much upon voice, our own and that of our informants, but we are also a discipline that must contemplate that inescapable presence in our practice which is an absence of voice. The virtue of the topic we treat here is that it makes us aware of how much may be neglected, by inadvertence or by design, in our work. In part this must be due to the very nature of mental processing, of concept formation, or of "the dynamic of the categorical"[20] itself. As much must be left unsaid as said, unheard as heard, unconceived as conceptualized. Our communicative interaction seems inevitably to rely upon and even need parsimony. It is obliged to neglect or silence as much as it attends to. The paradox of thinking lies in the fact that we must obviate, ignore, or silence so much of the virtually boundless stimuli of experience in order to focus, to be able to *pay attention* and to give salience and save ourselves from distraction. Otherwise we would ourselves be reduced to silence, like Borges's famous Funes the Memorious, silenced because he could not forget and could not silence the claim to his attention of any and all things that flooded into his experience. All was remembered and everything had to be attended to, to the point of stultification.

So while we seek in our ethnographies to give the breath of life to many voices we are ironically also inevitably neglectful of many others. At the same time, however, and in all honesty we have to recognize that the topic as we take it up here is important for us if only to remind us of the many silencings that accompany our practice. Lest we presume to have fashioned God's Truth in our narrative ethnographies, we need to be regularly reminded of how much of what we have committed to our final notes and to the ethnographic narrative that contains them has been perspectival and serendipitous and often enough quite brusquely selective. Ethnography is always an exercise in giving voice, to be sure, but it is also an exercise in displacing into anonymity many other possible voices. The challenge of ethnographic inquiry may rest out of our participant observation with the composition of that final ethnography which we manage to bring forth and get heard in text or image or both. But the challenge to ethnographic understanding lies in contemplating and attempting once more to evoke and meditate upon the many silences that surround it. These voices of silence, long lost or forgotten and unheard as they may be, once they are recalled again, may well become the more significant and perhaps the sweeter for having been at first or so long neglected or unheard. Treating once again what is long buried in file notes or what can come again in these evanescent "head notes," treating, that is, the subject of silence is a salutary exercise in the re-evocation of the plenitude of ethnographic inquiry and the silences imposed or ordained, advertent or inadvertent out of which its final forms must necessarily arise. But with this overdetermined and deliberate deafness we need not necessarily be foreverafter complicit. Reflecting on silence, as I believe and have argued, by returning us to attend to lost voices teaches us that humble lesson of *recognized partiality* by which we may more truly understand the challenges of our calling.

Notes

1. Cf. A. Aarne and S. Thompson, *The Types of the Folktale: A Classification and Bibliography*, Helsinki 1964. Among other Types, Type 886:(p.303) "The Girl who could not keep silent." And in Stith Thompsons's, "The Motifs of Silence and The Silent." *Motif Index of Folk Literature,* Bloomington,In.: Indiana University Press 1989, p.705.
2. Cf. Gregory Bateson's argument in "A Theory of Play and Fantasy," (In *Steps To an Ecology of Mind,* New York, 1972) that despite the many powers of creative and transposing expression that a fully open language gives to humans, and the many different things we can take an interest in and express, we still continue to be to a very large extent mainly interested, like the other higher animals, in our relationships with others.
3. Michel-Rolph Trouillot, *Silencing the Past: power and the production of history,* Boston, Mass: Beacon Press, 1995.
4. Ginzburg, Carlo, *The cheese and the worms : the cosmos of a sixteenth-century miller,* Penguin, 1982.
5. Natalie Zemon Davis, *The return of Martin Guerre,* Harvard: Cambridge, 1983.

6. Robert Darnton, *The great cat massacre and other episodes in French cultural history*, New York: Basic Books, 1984.
7. Begoña Aretxaga, "Terrorism as Thrill: First Thoughts on the War on Terrorism," in Gautam Ghosh (Ed.), "Civilization, Vulnerability and Translation: Reflections in the Aftermath of September 11th," *Anthropological Quarterly*, Vol. 75 (1) Winter 2001: pgs. 139-149.
8. Margaret Mead, personal communication.
9. Raymond D. Fogelson, "Schneider Confronts Componential Analysis," in R. Feinberg and M. Ottenheimer, *The Cultural Analysis of Kinship: The Legacy of David M. Schneider*, Urbana: U. Illinois Press. 2001. Pgs. 33-45.
10. Thomas Kuhn, *The Structure of Scientific Revolutions*, Chicago, 1996 (1970).
11. Particularly by Barbara Frankel, *Two Roshomon Effects and the Puzzled Ethnographer: On the Epistemology of Listening to Different voices*, Unpub. Ms. 1981; and by Karl Heider, "The Roshomon Effect: When Anthropologists Disagree," *American Anthropologist*, Vol. 90, 1988:73-81.
12. What Frankel calls Roshomon I. (differences due to perspective) and Roshomon II (plainly contradictory accounts more difficult to assess).
13. Although the whole purpose of Frankel's essay is to increase self-awareness in the ethnographer of Roshomon effects in his or her final "construal," she is also concerned to create a scale or measure of credibility involving the ethnographer in much soul searching. Heider for his part, in his later piece on Roshomon, is focused rather on disagreements in the ethnographic literature in the stories that anthropologists tell about their culture, as, for example the well known disagreement between Robert Redfield and Oscar Lewis over the Mexican village of Tepotzlan. He gives us a valuable listing of the four basic ways that can cause ethnographic disagreement and, in respect to Way 4, perspectival differences, the ten ways that might account for ethnographers looking differently at the same culture.
14. Renato Rosaldo, "From the door of his tent: the fieldworker and the inquisitor," in: Clifford, J. & Marcus, G.E., editors. *Writing culture: the poetics and politics of ethnography*, Berkeley: University of California Press, 1986.
15. For a classic account of the breakdown of a close field relationship into a fit of pique and consequent silence and its moral implications in a world so profoundly divided between the haves and the have-nots see, C. Geertz, "Thinking as a Moral Act" *The Antioch Review*.
16. J.W. Fernandez, *Bwiti: An Ethnography of the Religious Imagination in Africa*, Princeton: Princeton University Press, 1982. Pgs. 11-23.
17. Now deposited in the Africana Collection of the Herskovits Library of Northwestern University.
18. This is the term employed in the important collections of articles on this central activity of anthropologists, edited and perceptively guided by Roger Sanjek, *Fieldnotes:the Makings of Anthropology*. Ithaca: Cornell University Press, 1990.
19. See Foto 2 in the second photo signature insert between pages 454 and 455 of Bwiti: An Ethnography of the Religious Imagination in Africa (1982).
20. J.W. Fernandez, "Culture and Transcendent Humanization: On the Dynamic of the Categorical," *Ethnos*, 59 (3-4): 143-167, 1994.

References Cited

Aarne, A. and S. Thompson. 1964. *The Types of the Folktale: A Classification and Bibliography,* Helsinki: Folklore Fellows.

Aretxaga, Begoña. 2001. "Terrorism as Thrill: First Thoughts on the War on Terrorism." In Ghosh Gautam ed, *Civilization, Vulnerability and Translation: Reflections in the Aftermath of September 11th.* In *Anthropological Quarterly.* Vol 75 No 1. 150-154.

Bateson, Gregory. 1972. *Steps To an Ecology of Mind,* New York.: Ballantine.

Borges, Jorge Luis. 1962. "Funes the Memorious." in John Sturrock, ed., *Ficciones.* New York: Grove Press.

Darnton, Robert. 1984. *The Great Cat Massacre and Other Episodes in French Cultural History,* New York: Basic Books.

Davis, Natalie Zemon. 1983. *The Return of Martin Guerre,* Harvard: Cambridge.

Fernandez, James W. 1982. *Bwiti: An Ethnography of the Religious Imagination in Africa,* Princeton: Princeton University Press. Pgs 11-23.

_____. 1994. "Culture and Transcendent Humanization: On the Dynamic of the Categorical," *Ethnos,* 59 (3-4): 143-167.

Fogelson, Raymond D. 2001, "Schneider Confronts Componential Analysis." In R. Feinberg and M. Ottenheimer, eds., *The Cultural Analysis of Kinship: The Legacy of David M. Schneide.,* Urbana: University of Illinois Press. pp. 33-45.

Frankel, Barbara. 1981. *Two Roshomon Effects and the Puzzled Ethnographer: On the Epistemology of Listening to Different voices,* Unpub Ms. 65 pgs.

Geertz, Clifford. 1968. "Thinking as a Moral Act : Ethical Dimensions of Anthropological Fieldwork in the New States." *The Antioch Review* v.28 no.2 pp. 139-159

Ginzburg, Carlo. 1982. *The Cheese and the Worms : The Cosmos of a Sixteenth-century Miller,* New York: Penguin.

Heider, Karl. 1988. "The Roshomon Effect: When Anthropologists Disagree." *American Anthropologist.* Vol 90:73-81.

Kuhn, Thomas. 1970, *The Structure of Scientific Revolutions.* Chicago: University of Chicago Press.

Rosaldo, Renato. 1986. "From the door of his tent : the fieldworker and the inquisitor." in: Clifford, J. & Marcus, G.E., editors. *Writing*

Culture: the Poetics and Politics of Ethnography, Berkeley: University of California Press., 77-97.

Sanjek, Roger. 1990. *Fieldnotes:the Makings of Anthropology.* Ithaca: Cornell University Press.

Thompson, Stith. 1989. "The Motifs of Silence and the Silent," *Motif Index of Folk Literature,* Bloomington,In.: Indiana University Press 1989, 705.

Trouillot, M-Rolph. 1995. *Silencing the Past: Power and the Production of History,* Boston:Beacon Press.

Contributors

Maria-Luisa Achino-Loeb teaches at New York University/Gallatin where she continues to develop courses on *silence*. She has conducted research with Waldensians and other minorities within religious groups. Her work has been published in *American Anthropologist,* and *Theory in Psychology,* among others. She currently co-chairs the Advisory Council of the Anthropology Section, New York Academy of Sciences.

Pauline Gardiner Barber is Associate Professor of Sociology & Social Anthropology at Dalhousie University, Halifax NS., Canada. She recently guest edited *Anthropologica* 46(2), has chapters in edited volumes with Broadview, Routledge, SUNY Press, and Ashgate, and is working on a monograph on Philippine Migration, Citizenship and Development.

William O. Beeman is Professor of Anthropology and Theatre, Speech and Dance at Brown University, and a professional opera singer. He is author of *Language, Status and Power in Iran* and co-author of *The Third Line: The Opera Performer as Interpreter.* His forthcoming book is *Die Meistersinger: Artistry and Cultural Identity in a German Opera Theatre.*

Sue Cook is a Senior Lecturer in Anthropology at the University of Pretoria. She has conducted research on genocide in Cambodia and Rwanda and more recently on urban vernaculars and traditional forms of governance in South Africa. Her publications include *Genocide in Cambodia and Rwanda: New Perspectives* (ed) (Transaction 2005) and "New Technologies and Language Change: Towards an Anthropology of Linguistic Frontiers" (*Annual Review of Anthropology* 2004).

James Fernandez is Professor Emeritus of Anthropology at the University of Chicago. He has taught previously at Princeton, Dartmouth and Smith. He has done fieldwork in Equatorial (Fang), Southeast (Zulu) and West Africa (Ewe and Fon), and in Northern Spain (Asturias).

Ann Kingsolver is an associate professor of anthropology, and directs the Latin American Studies Program, at the University of South Carolina. She has written *NAFTA Stories: Fears and Hopes in Mexico and the United States* (Lynne Rienner Publishers, 2001) and edited *More than Class: Studying Power in U.S. Workplaces* (SUNY Press Series in the Anthropology of Work, 1998).

Robin E. Sheriff is an Associate Professor of Anthropology at the University of New Hampshire. She is the author of *Dreaming Equality: Color, Race and Racism in Urban Brazil* (Rutgers University Press 2001) as well as a number of articles, including one on the topic of cultural censorship in *American Anthropologist.* Her work is based on a twenty-month period of residence in a shantytown in Rio de Janeiro.

Gerald Sider is Professor of Anthropology (Emeritus) at the Graduate Center and the College of Staten Island, CUNY, and Adjunct Professor of Anthropology (Honorary) at Memorial University of Newfoundland. His two recent books are *Between History and Tomorrow: Making and breaking everyday life in rural Newfoundland* (1993) and *Living Indian Histories: Lumbee and Tuscarora peoples in North Carolina.* (1993). He is presently working on a book on the long history of suicide and substance abuse among the Innu and Inuit of Labrador, and on a book of collected essays.

Author Index

E

F

G

H

I

J

K

L

M

O

P

Q

R

S

T

V

W

Y

Z

Subject Index

D

E

F

G

H

I

J

K

L

M

N

O

P

R